KU-289-199

E. G. Gilbert was until recently the Royal Horticultural Society's Fruit Officer at Wisley, where from 1951 to 1968 he was in charge of extensive plantations and collections of hardy fruits as well as advisory and teaching work. In 1968 he moved to Long Ashton Research Station to take over the duties of Plantations Officer. Here a much larger acreage of hardy fruits and other crops is maintained for use in connexion with the extensive research programme of the Station.

Born in 1925 near Launceston, Mr Gilbert is a West Countryman whose early training in North Wales was interrupted by war service. After further training at the John Innes Institute, then situated at Merton, he went as a student to Wisley in 1948, completed the course and joined the Staff in 1950. Next year he became Fruit Officer and gained much early experience by working alongside the National Fruit Trials until they were transferred to Kent in 1954. He holds the National Diploma of Horticulture.

Mr Gilbert who lives in Long Ashton is married and has three children. His name is already associated with this series of handbooks, for he undertook the adaptation of Raymond Bush's original Penguins, *Apples*, and *Pears, Quinces and Stone Fruits*, into one volume – *Tree Fruit Growing*.

E. G. Gilbert

Soft Fruit
Growing

 Penguin Books

80p

Penguin Books Ltd, Harmondsworth,
Middlesex, England
Penguin Books Inc., 3300 Clipper Mill Road,
Baltimore, Md 21211, U.S.A.
Penguin Books Australia Ltd, Ringwood,
Victoria, Australia

First published 1970
Copyright © E. G. Gilbert 1970

Made and printed in Great Britain by
Butler & Tanner Ltd, Frome and London
Set in Monotype Times Roman

This book is sold subject to the condition that
it shall not, by way of trade or otherwise, be lent,
re-sold, hired out, or otherwise circulated without
the publisher's prior consent in any form of
binding or cover other than that in which it is
published and without a similar condition
including this condition being imposed on the
subsequent purchaser

Contents

Preface

This book is an attempt to present a straightforward but detailed account of soft-fruit growing for the amateur. Much of what it contains is well known and basic to the subject, but where appropriate I have tried to introduce helpful points from recent research and experimental work, as well as observations based on my own experience.

I am greatly indebted to the considerable number of people who have so willingly helped and advised me in the preparation of this book. In particular I must pay special tribute to Mr Brian Self, B.Sc., of East Malling Research Station, for much detailed and studied advice throughout, to his colleague Mr J. Goode, B.Sc., for details on the assessment and measurement of water requirements, and to the staff generally at East Malling.

I am also most grateful for all the help received from my colleagues at Wisley – to Mr C. D. Brickell, B.Sc., on botanical details, to Miss A. V. Brooks, B.Sc., for advice on diseases, to Mr K. M. Harris, B.Sc., on pests, to Mr R. P. Scase for his considerable assistance with photographs, and to Mr P. Walker for guidance on certain technical details. I am much indebted also to Mr E. W. Hobbis, B.Sc., for checking the chapter on blueberries, to Dr D. Wilson, B.Sc., Ph.D., of Long Ashton Research Station, for similarly assisting with that on strawberries, and to Mr H. R. Tuffin for checking that on vines.

Grateful acknowledgement is made to Mr J. E. Downward and his staff for providing many of the illustrations, including the cover; to East Malling Research Station for plates 9, 33 and 48; to the late Mr D. E. Green, M.Sc., for plate 50; to Long Ashton Research Station for plates 4, 16 and 25; and to the Shell Photographic Unit for plates 3, 21, 30, 31 and 49. Due acknowledgement is also made of the Crown copyright of plates 5 and 12.

I would in conclusion like to thank Mr Patrick Synge, the general editor, for his wise counsel and help in the final preparation of the manuscript. Equally appreciated is the help given by Mr Synge's assistant, Miss E. Napier.

Introduction

There is something about fruit-growing that is both rewarding and, at the same time, somewhat frustrating. Yet there is always the occasional season in which everything seems to crop in profusion and we marvel at the amount of fruit even a small bush can produce. The purpose of this book is to describe simply but in detail the cultivation of the soft fruits. Some of these are popular and widely grown; others are less so, yet interesting and valuable in their own right. Certain cultural requirements are common to all, or nearly all, the crops dealt with, but with such a wide range of plant types there are, naturally enough, individual likes and dislikes.

Rapid changes are taking place in methods of fruit-growing, and the wise fruit-grower will try to keep abreast of them and adopt new and proved techniques. Though many of these originate from research and experimental stations, there is something to be gained in experimenting on one's own. The gardener with a new plot is apt to ask, 'Which strawberry should I grow?' Depending on how many experts he asks, he is likely to get just as many different answers! The best and most interesting course to take would be to grow a few plants of a number of the leading cultivars (varieties) rather than several rows of one. This will soon answer his problem: he can choose the most successful for wider planting. Soft fruits, quick-cropping and with relatively small demands on space, are particularly suited to this approach.

1 · Soft Fruits in the Garden

Although we may envy those who live in sunnier parts we should, in some respects, be grateful for our own climate. The range of crops that it enables us to grow is indeed remarkable. We are apt to take many of them for granted, because they are available for most of the year, or over a considerable season. Others, however, seldom fail to whet the appetite with their fleeting and colourful appearance; in this category, most certainly, belong our soft fruits.

Definition

The term 'soft fruits' is a collective one generally used with reference to strawberries, raspberries, loganberries and other hybrid berries, blackberries, blackcurrants, red and white currants, gooseberries and blueberries. Currants, gooseberries and, more recently, blueberries are known as bush fruits; raspberries, blackberries, loganberries and allied hybrids are cane fruits. Grapes (a short chapter on which is included, p. 153) are in a class by themselves but can also conveniently be listed under the general heading 'soft fruits'.

The Value of Crops

With few exceptions all of these fruits are hardy under our climatic conditions and can be grown quite successfully in most gardens with a little care and attention. In general, it should be possible to gather valuable crops from the same plantation for a number of years before having to think of replacements. Black-currant bushes, for instance, can remain in healthy, vigorous production for at least eight years – even for fifteen and more under favourable conditions – while the useful life of red currants and gooseberries may be much longer.

Advantages of Soft Fruits

Soft-fruit growing has its pitfalls like everything else, though it should not be as puzzling or as complicated as many people seem to find it. Compared with tree fruits, for instance, the soft fruits can be relied upon to keep their place and not outgrow their station. Most of them are self-fertile, while tree fruits frequently are not; soft fruits can be protected from birds fairly easily: tree fruits often cannot; they can be sprayed very easily: tree fruits often cannot; they succeed in most areas: tree fruits may not, and so on. . . . This, of course, is exaggerating the case against tree fruits, but it does highlight some of the reasons why soft fruits should be much more widely grown than they are. People would then *know* what really fresh strawberries or raspberries taste like, for today there must be thousands who don't. However good the fruiterer or greengrocer, there is no substitute for home-grown produce, and in particular home-grown soft fruits.

The Importance of Planning

The first consideration is, of course, the size of the garden or allotment and the proportion of it one is willing to devote to soft fruits. Where space is no problem, most of the soft fruits can be tried, but with small gardens this is seldom possible. Strawberries are likely to be the first on any list. They are the one soft fruit for which fresh, healthy plants have to be planted regularly to produce consistent results. Because of this it is best to fit them in with the vegetable plot, where good fertile soil is always available for fresh planting. Good results can sometimes be obtained from an area permanently earmarked for strawberries, but where possible this is best avoided.

Next in popularity come raspberries and blackcurrants. These, with blackberries, loganberries and other hybrid berries, red and white currants, gooseberries and blueberries, should be looked upon as permanent crops, likely to occupy the ground for up to ten years, and often more. All these fruits have one thing in common – bird damage. Not only the fruits themselves but in the case of currants and gooseberries the overwintering buds as well are subject to it. How much simpler, then, to group them together in one area so that they can be protected in one block (Pl. 1). The size of the garden does not matter here so long as a simple plan is adhered to – namely, to reserve an area for whatever fruit it is decided to grow, and to use it for nothing else.

Apart from ease of protection from birds, grouping the fruits together means that they can be cared for properly. Manuring and spraying can be carried out as required and better and more

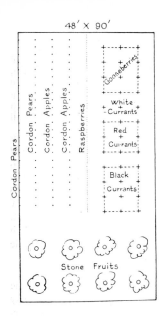

48' x 90'

Cordon Pears

Cordon Pears

Cordon Apples

Cordon Apples

Raspberries

Gooseberries

White Currants

Red Currants

Black Currants

Stone Fruits

1. Plan of one of the model fruit gardens at Wisley, showing how the soft fruits are laid out.

consistent cropping may well result. Fruit bushes are very often underplanted with bulbs or crowded out by flowers and vegetables which rob them of plant foods and moisture. This is a near certain way to disappointment, not only with fruit but with other crops as well. It is impossible to feed trees and bushes properly if the surrounding soil is cluttered with other plants; it may be equally impossible to do essential spraying if other crops are too close. And whether we like it or not, an occasional spray is *essential* if our efforts are to be rewarded.

Protection from Birds

There are a number of materials useful for protecting fruit crops from birds, but netting, in one form or another, is the best, in fact the only, answer (Pl. 20, p. 82). Pieces of old curtain or muslin may do for an odd bush, but something better is necessary for any quantity of fruit.

Until recently either repaired fish nets or new cotton or yarn nets have been the standard materials for temporary protection. Both are frequently advertised. It is well to remember that fish nets often have a diamond-shaped mesh. This means that pulling the net to its maximum length considerably reduces its width, while to gain more width the length is reduced, and allowance has to be made for this in calculating the amount required for a given area. New nets with a square mesh are easier to reckon with, as their measurement is fixed, but they are sometimes much dearer to buy, depending on the grade of material used.

Fruit nets are also now available made from synthetic substances such as nylon and polypropylene. Some of these are only a little more expensive than new heavy-grade cotton or yarn nets, and with correct treatment it is claimed that they last considerably longer. However, strong sunlight shortens their life unless they are dipped annually in a special preservative. More recently still, other brands of plastic netting have been put on the market. It would be of great benefit if a net possessing lasting strength and durability could be manufactured to retail at a reasonable price.

SIZE OF MESH. The smaller the mesh the dearer the net, the larger the mesh the greater the risk of small birds forcing a way in. In most cases one would be safe in choosing a three-quarter-inch mesh for soft fruits. If, on the other hand, the netting is to be used to cover tree fruits later in the season, particularly apples and pears, then the mesh may have to be half an inch. This is usually effective against small tits which cause havoc to ripening apples and pears but are far less interested in soft fruits. It is infuriating to watch these intelligent creatures search for a point where the mesh is fractionally larger. The net being pliable, they can force their way through and for this reason a half-inch mesh is the answer. For wire-netting, however, the three-quarter-inch mesh is quite satisfactory, since it will not bend to the birds' shape.

FRUIT CAGES. Even a simple arrangement of a few posts and cross canes can take valuable time to erect, and to this must be added the placing in position of the net afterwards. However the latter process can be made very much easier by using posts of a fairly small diameter, so that jam jars can be dropped over the top of them. The net then runs smoothly over the jars without any hitches or tears and the job is done in a quarter of the time. An alternative is to tie a piece of polythene over the post tops. If finances allow, one may well think in terms of a permanent enclosure or fruit cage. In this case the sides only should be permanent, the roof either being completed with ordinary fish or nylon nets when protection is needed, or being in the form of a series of removable panels. An excellent alternative is to mount the roof netting on a piece of alkathene piping; it can then be rolled on and off very easily.

A completely and permanently enclosed cage is inadvisable, as it deters pollinating insects from entering during the blossom period and it excludes birds for long periods during which many of them can be helpful by feeding on soil and insect pests. The permanent sides should be of a strong, durable material such as wire-netting. Ready-made sectional cages are sold by some of the larger sundries firms and net-makers.

The fruit cage is of particular value where there is serious bird damage to fruit buds in winter. In such cases the bushes need protection from November to March, inclusive. Add to these five months the period during which the fruit is ripening and it will be seen that protection is necessary for more than half the year.

The winter period of protection is one during which heavy snowfall can occur, and the collapse of hundredweights of snow caught by a flimsy net roof can smash fruit bushes beyond repair. Therefore, either remove the roof nets temporarily if snow threatens, or alternatively make the roof and its supports sufficiently strong to withstand heavy snowfall.

WIRE-NETTING ROOFS. The use of wire-netting for roofing in fruit cages is often questioned, and rightly so. Owing to chemical reaction, water dripping from the galvanized netting can scorch foliage underneath, more particularly in industrial areas where the atmosphere is heavily polluted and when the netting is rusty. Similar effects are sometimes seen on street trees standing beneath telephone wires.

THE CARE OF FRUIT NETS. Like everything else, fruit nets cost money and should therefore be looked after. Coil them up tidily and tie them so that they are easily and immediately ready for re-use, after first ensuring that they are thoroughly dry. Storing in a damp condition or in a damp place will severely curtail their useful life, particularly those made of cotton and yarn. Nylon and polypropylene, as already mentioned, are more vulnerable to

13

bright sunlight, so that once crops are gathered such nets should be removed.

Successional Cropping

The soft-fruit season is at best a short one, but reference to any list of cultivars (varieties) will show that we can do much to extend it by planting more than one kind of each fruit. To take two examples: the strawberry season can be considerably prolonged by using two varieties like 'Cambridge Rival' (early) and 'Talisman' (late mid-season). Blackcurrants can likewise be available over a much longer period by choosing a combination such as 'Boskoop Giant' (early), 'Wellington XXX' (mid-season) and 'Baldwin' (late). Picking would start in late June and continue into August, perhaps even later. This surely is much more convenient not only for the gardener but also for those in the kitchen. Plan to avoid gluts, not to make them.

Lack of Success

It is unfortunate that of all garden crops soft fruits are often the *least* rewarding, but failures are nearly always due to our own mistakes. The reasons for failure are numerous. The outstanding ones would certainly include:

Failure to select a suitable site
Lack of preparation before planting
Failure to obtain strong, healthy plant material
Failure to prune, or incorrect pruning
Failure to feed regularly, if at all
Failure to apply one or two basic and essential sprays for use against common pests and diseases

The remedies are mostly simple, and are all fully discussed in the ensuing chapters. Even as confusing an operation as pruning can be surprisingly interesting once the method has been understood.

2 · Sites and Soils

Sites

Whereas soils may be improved to the point where good crops can be grown, much still depends on the site itself and the general aspect of the garden. It is true that soft fruits can succeed in nearly all areas of the British Isles, but everyone knows how conditions vary in the same locality.

Frost Risk

This is a real and perennial hazard every fruit grower and gardener has to face. Something that is not generally realized is that the sheltered valley site carries the greatest frost risk. It may be sheltered from cold winds, but the spring frosts which damage fruit are always worse in low-lying areas. This is because on still, clear nights cold air flows down to the lowest level, just as cold water will. The longer the night, the severer the frost. There are frequent examples in late spring of gardens situated on a hillside escaping serious damage whereas less fortunate neighbours on lower slopes suffer extensive losses. This type of frost is known as a radiation frost and can occur on cloudless nights in most months of the year. The hard frosts of winter, when the whole air mass is freezing are usually of little danger to soft fruits, which are safely dormant at this time. However losses under severe winter conditions can occur in loganberries and some of the other hybrid berries.

Guarding against Frost

It is much easier to protect soft fruits against frost, as it is against birds, if they are grouped together. The fruits most likely to suffer spring frost damage are those which break into growth and flower early. They include all the currants, gooseberries and strawberries. It is the flowers that are particularly vulnerable, but if the frost is a bad one quite large fruits can be spoilt too. Luckily raspberries, blackberries and allied fruits do not normally flower until late May to June. By then all reasonable risk of damaging frost has passed in most areas, so if a garden is known to be especially bad for frost there are at least some soft fruits that can be counted on.

The best method of frost protection is undoubtedly some form of cover which can quickly be placed in position for the night as and when required. Hessian or old curtains are ideal, and with the aid of a few posts and wires can be used to cover some of the choicer and more valuable crops. Even a double layer of fish netting or sheets of newspaper can give some protection. Any such temporary structure should be sufficiently strong to withstand a sudden wind – a collapse may lead to considerable damage.

But the covering and uncovering of an area of any size is not usually practicable. This being so, there are one or two other measures that can help to reduce the risk of frost damage. Firstly, it is known that a wet soil loses heat to the atmosphere more slowly than a dry one. It is also a fact that the spring is usually the driest period of the year. Thus, where water is available, keep the ground moist and in so doing you will reduce the frost risk. Secondly, keep the ground firm. This allows heat to escape from the soil more freely than through loose cultivated ground and thus temper the cold air just above. Mulching too early with manure and compost has the same effect as a loose surface, so it may pay to delay any such applications in gardens known to be frosty. Yet again, weed-covered or grass-covered soil is more prone to frost than clean ground, because, like mulch, they act as a blanket and hamper the escape of warmth from the soil underneath. Straw can have exactly the same disadvantage on strawberry beds if put down too early.

There is yet another possible method of frost protection now practised by some fruit growers, though it may not be a practical proposition in the average garden. This is the use of a continuous mist-like spray of water for as long as the frost lasts.

Wind

Next to frost, wind is the most serious weather hazard, in particular cold winds from north and east. Not only are young shoots blown off – this can be disastrous on young red currants and gooseberries – but pollinating insects are discouraged from making their usual sorties. In consequence there is a general lack of pollination and poor crops may result. However, this problem

16

2. Gooseberry with drawn, one-sided growth due to the proximity of trees.

can usually be overcome. Hedges and fences can be made very attractive, besides giving shelter. Where space permits, plantings of ornamental trees and shrubs make excellent windbreaks and the whole garden may benefit from the resulting warmer and generally more amiable growing conditions.

Draughts

Even though a garden may for the most part be sheltered, it usually has its draughty corners. Few trees or plants thrive in such positions, and soft fruits are no exception. Narrow strips of ground between houses are typical man-made wind 'tunnels', and blocking them by a cross-wall, fence or hedge should benefit the garden.

Excessive Shade

Too much shade will invariably lead to disappointing results (Pl. 2). Where large trees overshadow a garden excessive shade is not the only problem, since trees also take all the nourishment and the soil is liable to dry out very quickly. A certain amount of shade, on the other hand, can be tolerated, although quality and flavour may suffer in consequence. As an example, a north-facing border against a wall or fence can be used for currants, gooseberries and loganberries, but the general quality and appearance of the fruit would not normally match that of crops grown in full sun.

Walls and Fences

The use of walls and fences for growing trained fruit trees is quite widespread, but the results are even more attractive if the same is done with soft fruits, particularly where space in the garden itself is restricted. The aspect should preferably, but not necessarily, be a sunny one; it must certainly not be draughty, for the reasons already stated. Red and white currants and gooseberries are ideal for training as cordons or fans against low structures or between fruit trees on larger walls. Blackberries, loganberries, other hybrid berries, and of course grapes are also excellent for wall training, but for these the area must be large enough. The various trained forms are well worth considering, for apart from saving space, they frequently produce larger and better-coloured fruits than their counterparts in the open garden. Detailed accounts of various trained forms are given in the appropriate chapters.

Upland Sites

No hard and fast forecast can be given on the possibilities of successful soft-fruit growing in upland areas. With strong winds and with cool, or even cold, summer temperatures it is usually difficult to achieve success especially over 600 ft. Nevertheless a little shelter can make all the difference – always assuming that soil conditions are favourable. Strawberries and raspberries should certainly be tried, and also gooseberries and blueberries.

One thing is certain – the only sure way of finding out is to try. Use a few plants of each sort. Two or three seasons' results should provide the answer.

Soils

It is no use providing an ideal site if it is not to be backed up with good soil. All our well-known soft fruits must have well-manured fertile ground if they are to succeed, the only exception being the more recently introduced American blueberry, which will thrive on thin, sandy, acid soils, providing adequate mulches of peat and compost are applied to conserve moisture.

Older houses often have the advantage of kitchen-garden soil that has been worked and enriched for many years, and providing it is maintained in this condition it should be ideal for soft fruits. The gardens of new houses, on the other hand, may suffer the serious disadvantage of possessing little or no good top soil, and it is particularly in these instances that extra care is needed. Until the existing soil has been built up, or possibly replenished with some good loam, reasonable returns cannot be expected. Besides fresh soil, every effort should be made to introduce as much humus-forming material as possible – rotted farmyard manure, compost, peat, leafmould, anything that will assist in building up fertility. This will take time, and it is probably wisest to use the ground for short-term crops such as vegetables for a year or two, particularly those like potatoes which require generous manuring, before trying soft fruits in any quantity. If manure and compost are in short supply, be generous with them on a small plot rather than trying to spread a little over the whole garden.

Soils vary greatly and special points to watch for on the different types may be summarized as follows:

Clay Soils

Providing they are satisfactorily drained, clay soils can produce really heavy crops of first-rate quality. The danger of waterlogging should never be forgotten, however, for it only needs one wet winter to cause considerable losses, as many found to their cost in 1960–61. Raspberries in particular will not tolerate excessive wetness, nor will strawberries. Indeed, there are few crops that will withstand wet conditions on badly drained clay soil for long. Moreover, when the other extreme is reached and clay soil lies baked and dried out, it develops deep crevices which can tear the roots apart.

The friability and general texture of a clay soil can be improved by liming where permissible (see p. 21) and by applying peat, coarse sand, grit and bulky organic manures. A marked improvement, however, may take several years of hard work. It will always remain clay, at best a difficult type of soil to cultivate, but with perseverence it can often be made into a workable one.

Sands and Gravels

These may be the easiest soils to dig and work generally, but they are usually poor, hungry and soon dry out, even in a normal summer, and usually at a time crucial to the development of fruit. Lack of humus is the trouble, and constant heavy dressings of *well-rotted* manure and compost, plus any other humus material, are vital here. Building up the humus not only supplies much-needed food reserves but also enables the soil to hold considerably more moisture. Light sandy-gravelly soils may encourage earliness, since they warm up more quickly than heavier ground. It should be remembered, however, that they also lose heat quickly. They are inclined, therefore, to increase any frost risk, not only because temperatures above them will be colder but also because crops may well be further advanced and thus more vulnerable to frost.

Loams

The loams are capable of producing the best fruit of all. Loam is a general term applied to a considerable range of soils which have in common a reasonable percentage of humus or organic matter. Thus there are clay loams which tend to be on the heavy side, medium loams which are less heavy, and sandy loams which are considerably lighter but which still contain more humus than the really sandy or gravelly ground. The one thing to remember is that even a good loam will not last for ever and to get the best results from it crops must be adequately fed.

Chalk and Limestone Soils

These, like the loams, can vary a great deal. Where chalk or limestome comes to within eighteen inches of the surface and the top soil is poor, fruit-growing may well prove difficult, but if there is a reasonable depth of good soil then prospects are much brighter. Lack of humus is again the problem. This must be compensated for by giving liberal dressings of rotted farmyard manure and similar humus-forming material, firstly when preparing for planting and afterwards as an annual mulch. Without it results may be very disappointing.

On chalk and limestone soils there is a distinct risk that soft-fruit plants – and many others besides – will suffer from the effects of deficiencies of iron or manganese, possibly both.

Foliage loses its healthy green colour and growth may be much weakened in consequence (see p. 43). It is largely because of the risk of such trouble that annual mulching is so valuable on these soils. It creates a fertile surface layer and a reserve of moisture in which roots can form and from which essential nutrients can be extracted. In this way the ill-effects of the natural soil may be lessened.

Soil pH and the Use of Lime

The indiscriminate use of lime can do much more harm than good. The incidence of certain deficiencies on chalk soils that has just been underlined is caused by the presence of too much calcium. Over-liming may create precisely the same problem.

The fact is that most crops, including all soft fruits and tree fruits, prefer slightly acid soil conditions. The gardener cannot know for certain whether his soil needs lime or not without a simple soil test. Inexpensive testing kits are available, but it is often more satisfactory to get a sample tested where possible through one's county authorities. The degree of acidity or alkalinity of a soil is expressed technically as its pH. The figure of pH 7 is taken as neutral, values above this denoting alkaline or 'limey' soils and those below denoting acid soils. Thus a pH of 8 would be distinctly alkaline, whereas one of pH 7·2 would be only slightly alkaline. A pH of 4 would be very acid, whereas pH 6·5 would be only slightly acid, and so on. For soft fruits a pH of 6·0 to 6·5 should be aimed at, though it should be lower for blueberries. Bearing this in mind, it is generally safe to recommend 4 oz. per sq. yd of ground chalk or limestone where soil pH is known to be 5·5 or less. If it is over pH 5·5, do not lime unless special circumstances and expert advice deem it to be essential. The value of obtaining an official soil test is that recommendations of lime requirements, based on the pH reading, are usually precisely stated.

The use of lime can help to improve the texture and general cultivation of difficult, heavy soils, particularly clay. But here again, the pH of the soil must first be determined to show how much lime, if any, can safely be applied. If indeed it is safe to do so it is best to use one of the cooler forms of lime such as ground chalk, spreading it at the prescribed rate and working it in well before planting.

Correcting Over-Limed Soils

Liming can quickly improve an over-acid soil, but unfortunately there is no such simple or rapid method available for reducing the ill-effects of over-limed soil. The long-term treatment must be first to incorporate, then to mulch with, plenty of humus-forming material such as farmyard manure, peat and compost and to avoid using fertilizers containing free lime such as Nitro Chalk and bone meal. Sulphate of ammonia (see p. 42) is well-known for increasing acidity and should be used for supplying nitrogen. Sequestrenes have recently been introduced (see p. 44). These are available in small packs and can be very effective, but they are expensive if any but small areas are to be treated.

Drainage

Adequate drainage is vital. One or two trial holes, 18–24 ins. deep, should soon indicate how near to the surface water is lying. Obviously the heavier soils, particularly clay, are the ones on which trouble is most likely. In borderline cases the possible ill-effects of constant wetness on a heavy soil may be offset by planting on slightly raised beds. If the surface is raised by 4 to 6 ins. above the general level of the garden, much of the root system will enjoy drier conditions. The only danger lies in greater susceptibility to drying-out in summer, but this can be avoided by timely mulching and watering. Any soil can be temporarily flooded following heavy rain, but the effects of excessively wet winters cannot always be foreseen, and bad drainage must be put right before planting. For small tracts of ground one or two tile drains placed in a trench 12 to 15 ins. deep with an outlet to a lower-lying ditch or drain is often adequate. For larger areas a herring-bone network of tile drains may have to be constructed. On this scale second thoughts may be necessary, and expert advice should be sought on site lest the possible expense incurred is not justified. Certainly on low-lying ground there may be a real problem in finding sufficient fall to carry the water away.

Watering

The value of watering soft fruits cannot be over-emphasized. Heavier crops of better quality are produced for a longer season; and growth is uninterrupted, so that the foundations are soundly laid for the following year's crop.

Considerable work has been done at East Malling Research

Station in Kent on the water requirements of soft fruits; the following details, which should enable readers to irrigate with reasonable precision rather than by guesswork, are a result of their work.

A good watering should apply the equivalent of one inch of rainfall at least, that is $4\frac{1}{2}$ gallons per sq. yd. The difficulty lies in knowing how much a particular sprinkler or spray line is supplying – in other words how long it should be left in one position to supply the equivalent of an inch of rainfall. The answer can be found in the following manner.

Invert the sprinkler to be used into a 2-gallon or 3-gallon bucket and switch the tap full on. Measure how long it takes to fill the bucket and repeat this two or three times to arrive at an average filling time. Once this is known, a fairly accurate assessment can be made. For example, it takes a sprinkler 20 seconds to fill a 2-gallon bucket. Thus the area wetted by the sprinkler would similarly receive 2 gallons for 20 seconds, or 6 gallons per minute. It only remains to calculate the area wetted by the sprinkler to find the time it must remain in one position to give $4\frac{1}{2}$ gallons per sq. yd. Thus if the sprinkler wets a circle of 4 yards' radius, the calculation is $22/7 \times 4 \times 4$ sq. yds (πr^2). This works out in round figures at 50 sq. yds. Therefore 50 sq. yds will need $50 \times 4\frac{1}{2}$ gallons to equal an inch of rain, or 225 gallons. It took 1 minute for the sprinkler to give 6 gallons, therefore it will take $225/6$ minutes, or $37\frac{1}{2}$ minutes, to water the 50 sq. yds.

In practice one would water for a more convenient time of 40 or 45 minutes, the extra few gallons being of no consequence. Equal distribution of the water over the whole area is unlikely (and with circular sprinklers the areas watered must overlap anyway) and it is therefore sensible to vary the siting of the sprinkler at each watering.

Some irrigation units will of course be more difficult than others to measure for output, but this should be possible by one means or another – perhaps using a bath or even polythene sheeting in lieu of a bucket. Obviously if the equipment waters an oblong strip, the calculation of area is simple. Moreover, strips of ground can be watered without the overlap that is bound to occur with circular areas.

Details concerning the watering of individual crops will be found in the chapters dealing with the crop in question.

3 · The Importance of Plant Health

Some soft fruits are unfortunately very prone to troubles which, although they may not be obvious initially, in the long term can be devastating. Garden-grown soft fruits may be retained for years without the owner realizing (a) that they are a waste of time for himself and (b) that they are a potential source of trouble to his neighbour's garden. The reference is of course to virus diseases.

How Viruses Spread

The control of virus diseases has to be by prevention, not cure. In many instances a virus is spread by a vector or carrier, and aphids ('greenfly') are often the culprits (Pl. 3). They feed by sucking sap, and if, for example, they feed on a virus-infected strawberry they automatically carry virus-ridden sap from that plant. Feeding on a healthy plant immediately 'injects' it with the 'poison' from the unhealthy specimen. In fact, the sequence is much the same as that whereby malaria is spread by mosquitoes.

3. Raspberry shoot heavily infested with rubus aphid, a vector of certain virus diseases which affect raspberries.

If the vector is known it must be controlled as effectively as possible to minimize the chances of virus infection. The important viruses of soft fruits are dealt with in the appropriate chapters, to which reference should be made, the purpose at this point merely being to explain simply the effects of viruses and how they are spread. By no means all of them are spread by insects, but some of the most important certainly are.

Once a plant is virus-infected it must not be used for propagating. Runners from an infected strawberry, suckers from an infected raspberry, cuttings from an infected blackcurrant (Pl. 4), will all suffer the same virus as the source from which they were taken. To use such material is a complete and utter waste of time. Yet this is the sort of risk that one may well run if the importance of virus diseases is not understood. If therefore you are in doubt about the health of soft fruits a lot of time and trouble can be saved by

(a) seeking expert advice, and

(b) destroying the plants if investigation shows this to be advisable.

How can one be certain of planting healthy replacements?

Buying Healthy Stock

Elaborate certification schemes are now operated by the Ministry of Agriculture for the production of clean young stock of straw-

4. Blackcurrant bush heavily infested with big bug mite, as the swollen rounded buds show. This pest is a vector of reversion virus in blackcurrants.

berries, raspberries, loganberries and blackcurrants, these being by far the most important soft-fruit crops. Other kinds of soft fruits may also carry viruses, but the effects are usually less severe and have not as yet justified the time and expense a certification scheme involves. Very briefly, young stock of strawberries, raspberries, loganberries and blackcurrants for certification may be raised only under rigid conditions. For instance, the source of supply of the plants or cuttings must be known to be virus-free, and a specified distance must separate them from other plantations of the same fruit.

It is not the purpose here to give lengthy details of the certification schemes for soft fruits, but merely to underline their existence so that gardeners may take full advantage of them. This can be done by purchasing certified plants from a firm advertising them to be so (if necessary the certificate number can be asked for) rather than relying on uncertified material. This applies above all to strawberries, in which the spread of virus can be rapid and devastating, not least because several different viruses are involved.

Horticultural publications contain advertisements of growers offering certified material, but if you are in any difficulty the publication editors, County Horticultural Education Authorities or County Advisers, The Royal Horticultural Society, etc., are always able to advise on suitable sources of supply. Where commercial crops are concerned, the Ministry of Agriculture's National Agricultural Advisory Service should be consulted.

Maintaining Healthy Stock

For best results with strawberries, certified runners should be bought every two or three years. Even so there are a number of simple, yet important, cultural practices that can help considerably in maintaining plant health generally:

(1) *Burning old virus-infected plants and bushes.* Do not fall to the temptation of retaining the old bed 'just for one more year' while the new, certified plants are becoming established. Unhealthy specimens are a constant source of danger and to plant fresh stock adjacent to them may well waste money.

(2) *Spraying to control aphids* ('*greenfly*'). Aphids are by no means the only virus vectors, but they are certainly one of the commonest (Pl. 3). They can be expected in greater or lesser numbers each season and their effective control, particularly on

strawberries, will greatly help to reduce the spread of virus (see p. 30).

(3) *Propagating only from healthy, fruitful plants*. This may seem obvious, but to retain stock that is not thriving as it should increases the risk that one will propagate from it.

(4) *Roguing*. This is merely a regular inspection of one's own plants and bushes to eradicate and burn weaklings and suspects – not just among old stock but new as well.

(5) *Maintaining hygiene and good cultivation*. Cleanliness and maintaining a fertile soil both affect the performance of plants. Weeds, for instance, may carry viruses and the vector of those viruses, so that their timely removal is advisable. Fertility of the soil means that strong growth is encouraged and the stronger and healthier a plant is the less likely it is to fall victim to ill health.

4 · Spraying

Spraying is a subject on which one must be prepared to use common sense. On the one hand there are those who denounce spraying in any shape or form, and on the other those who, if they had their way, would apply every spray in the book. Good practice lies between these two extremes.

Spray Materials for Garden Soft Fruits

Spray materials available to the amateur are numerous. Some are so well known that one is sufficiently certain how, when and for what they should be used. Others may mean nothing to most of us, and rather than use the wrong thing it is sound policy to seek *expert* advice on which material is best for any given pest or disease.

An inexpensive booklet, *Gardening Chemicals*, published by the Royal Horticultural Society, is a mine of information on precisely this subject, and lists the proprietary brand names under which the various formulations are sold. (It is available from The Secretary, R.H.S. Offices, Vincent Square, London, SW1, 7s. 6d. plus 9d. postage and packing.) A similar publication is the Ministry of Agriculture's *Chemicals for the Gardener* (from Her Majesty's Stationery Office, York House, Kingsway, London, WC2, 1s. 3d.). Both booklets emphasize the advisability of

5. Chemical Approvals Scheme label.

using only those materials that bear the Agricultural Chemicals Approval Scheme mark (Pl. 5).

The following lists contain some of the most reliable substances for use on soft fruits. (Proprietary brand names cannot conveniently be included and reference to the R.H.S. booklet mentioned above is advised on this point where doubt exists.)

Fungicides

BORDEAUX MIXTURE. This is one of the old-time fungicides and is a mixture of copper sulphate and lime. It is now available in convenient packs for easy mixing and is very useful against diseases such as cane spot and spur blight in raspberries and leaf spot in strawberries and blackcurrants.

CAPTAN. One of the safest and most effective modern sprays. Its chief use in soft fruits is against botrytis (grey mould) on strawberry fruits, but it must not be used on fruit destined to be preserved, as it causes taint (see p. 69).

COPPER (formulations other than Bordeaux mixture). Various other formulations of copper are available as an alternative to Bordeaux mixture and should be used as the makers' instructions indicate.

DICHLOFLUANID. This recently introduced fungicide controls botrytis on strawberries without danger of taint.

DINOCAP. Another eminently successful and safe modern spray material. It is effective against a wide range of powdery mildews, which among soft fruits include gooseberry mildew and strawberry mildew.

LIME SULPHUR. This is still a valuable alternative to the modern sprays that have largely superseded it. As yet it is the only preventive measure available to amateur gardeners against blackcurrant gall mite ('big bud' mite). Used against this pest it will also reduce the incidence of American gooseberry mildew on blackcurrants. Lime sulphur must be used with care, however, for some blackcurrant cultivars may be scorched by it at more than 1 per cent strength and yellow-fruited gooseberries should not be treated with it.

One point is worth noting – lime sulphur sprayed on black-currants will only help to prevent 'big bud'; it will *not* control any big bud mites already present.

THIRAM. A valuable fungicide for the control of botrytis on strawberries. Like captan however its use within three weeks of picking is not safe on fruit destined to be preserved because it causes taint.

WASHING SODA. It is not generally realized that this is a very useful material against gooseberry mildew (see Chapter 11, p. 148).

ZINEB. Zineb contains a zinc compound and can be used to control leaf spot on blackcurrants and gooseberries.

Insecticides

Generally speaking it is the insecticides that are, or can be, the dangerous sprays to use. To be effective they must *kill* insects and must therefore possess some poisonous or paralysing property. This, therefore, means that they should always be used with extra care.

BHC. This should *not* be used on soft fruit as it causes an unpleasant taint. Gamma–BHC can be used where advised.

DDT. DDT has become so well known and was used so indiscriminately that one tends to lose sight of the reasons for its effectiveness. It acts firstly as a stomach poison to insects and secondly as a contact poison. It is also very persistent. Because of this it should be used and treated with respect. Soft-fruit pests controlled by DDT include capsids, caterpillars (not gooseberry sawfly), strawberry blossom weevil and blackcurrant midge. Used indiscriminately DDT may encourage another pest to flourish which it does not control. Possible alternatives to DDT include trichlorphon, malathion and derris and these are much less persistent.

DERRIS. Derris is derived from plants, particularly *Derris* and *Lonchocarpus*, the active ingredient being rotenone. It is one of the safest insecticides but is less persistent and therefore less efficient than many of the modern spray materials, so that more frequent applications may be necessary to obtain an effective control. Derris-sprayed crops can be eaten the day after treatment. Pests controlled include aphids, gooseberry sawfly, caterpillars and the larvae of the raspberry beetle. The dust form will also control wasps.

DIMETHOATE. Formulations of this compound are now available to amateur gardeners. Their action is systemic, that is the spray is *absorbed* by the plant treated, so that sap-sucking insect pests like aphids and red spider are controlled. Such sprays must obviously be used carefully and a minimum of seven days is required between spraying and harvesting. (N.B.: Chrysanthemums must not be treated with dimethoate sprays.)

DNOC/PETROLEUM. It is advisable to avoid using this substance in gardens. It is distinctly unpleasant to handle and in concentrations of more than 5 per cent strength DNOC is classed as a Part II substance in the Ministry of Agriculture (Poisonous Substances) Regulations. The spray should at all times be kept from skin and eyes. Highly toxic both to humans and animals.

LIME SULPHUR. Used as a spray to prevent blackcurrant gall (big bud). See p. 112).

MALATHION. This is still one of the best garden sprays for aphids and is also effective against capsid bugs, the larvae of gooseberry sawfly and raspberry beetle and active stages of red spider mites. Only one clear day is needed between application and harvesting.

NICOTINE. A very old and well-known insecticide requiring just as much care and respect as many of the much-maligned modern sprays. In concentrate form it is very poisonous. Pests controlled include aphids, gooseberry sawfly larvae and capsid bugs. Two clear days are necessary between spraying and picking.

TAR OIL. This is a well-known and well-tried old favourite. It is applied in winter when plants are completely dormant and soft fruits that can be treated with it include currants, gooseberries, raspberries, loganberries and blackberries. Tar oil controls the over-wintering stages of aphids and some moths and has a general cleansing effect. Evergreen hedges, lawns, etc., should be protected from any spray drift as they may be scorched by it.

TRICHLORPHON. An organophosphorus insecticide with some of the properties of the older organochlorine insecticides such as DDT. It can be used as an alternative to DDT for the control of caterpillars.

Dangers and Precautions

All spray materials should be handled with sensible care. If this is done there is no reason for any alarm over them and the benefits they can bring can be gained without any trouble.

Simple rules to follow when handling spray materials are:

1. Follow the makers' instructions word for word. If in doubt about the safety of any spray on a particular crop seek expert advice first.

2. Use a pair of rubber gloves when handling and mixing sprays, particularly where this is indicated in makers' instructions. The gloves should be washed clean afterwards and not left contaminated with spray concentrate.

3. Do not smoke or eat while spraying or handling spray materials, particularly insecticides.

4. Do not inhale sprays and dusts.

5. In the event of concentrate being spilt on the skin, wash off immediately with cold water.

6. Wash hands and face thoroughly in soapy water immediately after spraying.

7. Wash and/or flush out all spray utensils after use, but *not* in butts or tanks used for watering plants.

8. Do not mix spray materials in confined, enclosed places. Equally, avoid mixing in windy conditions.

9. Avoid spray drift on to edible crops, and in small gardens have regard for neighbours' crops which might be contaminated. Spraying in still weather is advisable. Minimum intervals to

allow between spraying and picking are usually mentioned in the makers' instructions and for sprays and dusts listed above are as follows:

BHC	Use not advised on soft fruits
Captan	No clear period needed
DDT	14 clear days
Dichlofluanid	3 weeks
Dimethoate	7 clear days
Dinocap	7 clear days
Malathion	1 clear day
Nicotine	2 clear days
Thiram	7 clear days
Trichlorphon	2 clear days
Zineb	7 clear days

10. Lock all spray materials in a safe place away from children.

11. After thorough washing flatten and bury tin containers and bury bottles. Avoid contamination of ponds, waterways and ditches.

Sprayers

As soft fruits are all conveniently small and compact it should not be difficult to buy a reasonably priced, efficient sprayer for them. One of the hand-operated syringes, double-action hand sprayers or pressurized knapsack-type sprayers should be quite adequate (Pl. 6). Makes and patterns vary, but in the last category in particular new light-weight plastic containers represent a great advance from the old and cumbersome metal knapsack sprayers. Moreover, the plastic materials used are often transparent, so that it is simple to measure required amounts into the sprayer as well as to see how much of the mixture has been used. Where powered tools are used it is sometimes possible to buy a spray unit for use with the same tool. While the expense may not be justified for soft fruits alone, it may be so if fruit trees also are to be sprayed.

Do not necessarily buy the first syringe or sprayer you happen to notice. Excellent exhibits of sprayers and other garden equipment are to be seen at the larger horticultural and agricultural shows (e.g. Chelsea) and it often pays to try out and weigh up the different makes before making up one's mind. (See Pl. 6.)

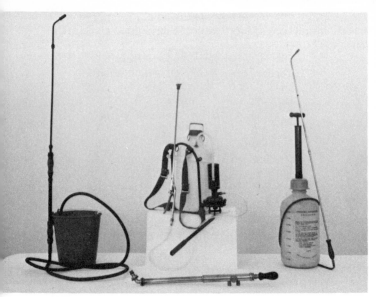

6. Sprayers suitable for garden soft fruits.

Practical Hints on Spraying

REGULAR TROUBLES. Some pests and diseases are an annual nuisance and for these the appropriate spray should be put on as a matter of routine. A typical example is gooseberry mildew, for which prevention is much easier than any cure. Other troubles which come into the same category include grey mould (botrytis) on strawberry fruits, raspberry beetle larvae in raspberry fruits and the various kinds of 'greenfly'. Equally important is the annual spraying of blackcurrants with lime sulphur to prevent any build-up of gall mite ('big bud'), since this pest is often a forerunner of the reversion virus.

BEES AND OTHER POLLINATING INSECTS. The general aim should be not to spray when plants and bushes are in flower, nor when bees are seen to be working. Spray-drift onto flowering weeds should also be avoided if possible.

DRY FOLIAGE. Sprays are mixed to a definite dilution which wet foliage will only weaken, possibly leading to little if any benefit from the spray applied.

CALM CONDITIONS. Excessive wind will lead to poor coverage and possibly a drift of poisonous spray on to edible crops.

HOT SUN. Spraying on hot, sunny days can lead to severe scorching of the foliage. To avoid this, spray in the late afternoon or early evening.

SPRAY COVERAGE. Slip-shod spraying is a waste of time and materials. Spray systematically up, down, around – not forgetting *under* the foliage, as well as the centre of thick bushes like gooseberries and blackcurrants. Quite a forceful spray is needed to penetrate strawberries, particularly in the control of aphids, which spread certain of the virus diseases.

USE OF WETTERS AND SPREADERS. Many proprietary sprays are produced complete with their own 'built-in' spreader, but if the addition of a wetting agent is advised then this should be done. Without it the spray will run into droplets on contact with foliage, resulting in inadequate coverage.

5 · Planting and Manuring

Correct planting and adequate manuring are vital for real success with soft fruits. Some general considerations on sites and soils have already been made in Chapter 2 (p. 15) and it is assumed that the garden is now in a clean and reasonably fertile condition. However, a fertile soil is of itself not capable of maintaining heavy crops indefinitely. It must be supplemented by regular applications of manures and fertilizers, varied to suit the needs of individual soils.

Preparation for Planting

Except for strawberries, the major soft fruits are fairly long-lived. Thus, for perhaps ten to fifteen years the only occasion on which manure can safely be dug *into* the soil is before planting. Mulching may be carried out in subsequent years – indeed should be – but results will not be the same if adequate pre-planting dressings have not been given. The practice of forking, sometimes even digging, through soft-fruit beds in the autumn or winter, possibly to incorporate manure, is a bad one, because not only is the soil loosened but, more important, many roots are laid bare and torn.

The preparation of a bed for any soft fruit should be started well in advance of planting, so that the soil has ample time in which to settle. If the ground is being used for vegetables it is advisable to clear them by July or August so that the bed can be dug over. Ideally it should be double-dug, but if it is known to be in good condition then thorough single-digging may be adequate. In either event really generous quantities of farmyard manure, compost, leafmould and the like should be incorporated. Coarser strawy material can be used on heavy ground to lighten it (see p. 19) but the lighter and more hungry soils need manure that is well rotted.

On really poor ground excellent results can be obtained by adding mushroom compost, always providing the reaction of the soil is sufficiently acid (pH 6·0 or less). This is manure that has been composted and used in a special way for mushroom production, hence its excellent value for the open garden. I have seen really sandy, stony ground produce fine fruit crops where heavy dressings of mushroom compost have been used before planting. It is also excellent for lightening heavy soils, though one must bear in mind that only the more acid soils should be dressed with it.

If manure or compost is in short supply, dressings of bone meal, hoof and horn meal and sulphate of potash should be applied a week or two before planting, by scuffling them into the top few inches. Bone meal and hoof and horn should each be given at 3–4 oz. per sq. yd and sulphate of potash at 1 oz. per sq. yd. But there is nothing to equal bulky manure and compost, and every effort should be made to obtain it.

Weedy Ground

Annual weeds are bound to occur and are no problem. They can easily be skimmed off the surface and turned in with the manure. It is the perennial weeds like couch grass, creeping thistle, convolvulus (bell-bind) and ground elder that must be avoided. The ground must be completely clear of these and their like; if not, a losing battle will be fought and plants and bushes will soon suffer.

The Use of Lime

This is fully discussed in Chapter 2 (p. 15). However, a reminder is perhaps advisable at this point because it is in the preparation before planting that lime should be given if tests show it to be necessary. On no account should it be applied indiscriminately, as on many soils this can lead to trouble (see p. 21).

Marking-Out

With the ground ready and prepared, mention must be made of the value of a planting plan (Pl. 1, p. 11). If only an odd bush or two are involved, this will not be necessary, but for any quantity of soft fruits it will save much time and trouble. The plan should be made *before* stock is ordered so that one knows exactly what quantity of each fruit is required and, more to the point, how it is to be fitted into the general garden layout. Using a piece of squared paper the plan can be prepared taking into account the planting distances necessary, how many bushes of each fruit are wanted, etc. The area can then be marked out with canes before

7. The bushes on the left have been heeled in, those on the right are in position for heeling-in.

planting, each bush or plant heeled in by its cane and the whole operation made considerably easier.

Newly Delivered Plants, Heeling-in, etc.

It is often not convenient to plant immediately on delivery. However, any delay can be damaging to plant roots, which dry out unless the proper precautions are taken. These are easy to satisfy. All that is required is that a simple trench be taken out (Pl. 7) into which the roots are carefully and adequately firmed (heeled in). If the ground is very wet a drier patch near a wall or fence should be used. In very cold conditions with hard frost it is probably best to keep the plants in their packing material undisturbed in a shed, with a little extra straw placed around each bundle, until milder conditions return.

Planting Time

Apart from strawberries, for which runners taken in August–September are ideal, the best time for planting is generally from late October onwards. The soil is then still comparatively warm and plants and bushes usually make a certain amount of root, so that they are already partly established when warmer spring weather arrives. But autumn planting is not always possible or preferable – maybe stock has not been ordered early enough or bad weather has delayed delivery or made the soil too wet. In fact there is nothing against later planting provided extra care is taken in the months immediately following. Indeed, one could plant as late as April and with adequate watering and pampering get away with it. This should not be done by choice, however, and every effort should be made to plant soft fruits by late February or early March. Currants and gooseberries in particular start growth during March, and to be moved at such a late stage cannot possibly do them any good. In any event, later plantings must be watched carefully – any check through lack of water in spring and early summer can make all the difference between good and poor results. A similar need for watering may well arise with strawberries planted in August–September.

The Planting Operation

Two conditions must be observed for successful planting. Firstly, the soil and the weather must be suitable. Soil that is too wet or sticky, or that has any hint of frost 'crust' on it, must be avoided and the plants heeled in as described above. Secondly, each plant must be placed in a planting hole which is both large enough and the correct depth (Pl. 8). It is surprising how many people unwittingly bundle a quart-sized root system into a pint-sized hole. Squeezed together in this way the roots will never function properly, and growth and general performance will suffer considerably in consequence. The hole should be wide enough to accommodate the full spread of the roots easily (with torn roots suitably trimmed) and with an inch or two to spare (Pl. 8). Again, bushes must be planted at the correct depth. The best guide for this is the existing nursery soil mark, which can often be seen and which shows the depth at which the plant or bush was growing in the nursery. In general, replant to the same position and you will not go far wrong.

The actual planting sequence for the bigger bushes deserves description, because to do it correctly requires more attention to detail than many realize. With a hole both large enough and deep enough the root system is carefully spread over the base of

8. A red currant bush in position for planting. The hole must allow ample room for the root system.

the hole. This should be slightly mounded and firmed so that the roots sit snugly without any cavities beneath them that could lead to unseen air pockets after the hole has been filled in. One then proceeds to cover the bottom-most roots with good top soil and to firm carefully. Root systems are often in layers (Pl. 8). Each layer should be spread out and covered *at its own level*, not bunched together and firmed in one operation. Lighter soils, in particular, require considerable, but careful, firming so that all roots are in close contact with the soil particles. Without this the effects of drought will be felt all the sooner, and growth will suffer. It is often a good practice, on heavier soils especially, to break down the sides of the planting hole before levelling off. This ensures that the soil is of even texture and compaction so that rapid and extensive root development is encouraged. Unbroken, rock-like sides in a planting hole may form a considerable physical barrier to roots on some soils.

One point to assist in planting on poor shallow soils: by the time the second spit is reached, often before it, sand and gravel may be apparent. In taking out the planting hole keep the good top soil in its own heap and then 'lose' the poorer subsoil over adjacent ground. When planting, fill in with good top soil only. This, together with adequate manure underneath, will go a long way to ensuring success.

Manuring Soft Fruits

The feeding of soft fruits is one of those vital points that are often forgotten. The importance of heavy manuring in the preparation before planting has already been emphasized, but this is only half the story. Such dressings, together with the nutrients already held by the natural soil, may well sustain and produce good crops for a year or two, but if they are not soon supplemented by surface feeding results will fall off.

Mulching

The manure and fertilizer requirements of soft fruit plants are really quite straightforward. A manure and/or compost heap is the first choice – results prove over and over again that the sensible use of rotted farmyard manure and compost dug in before planting and as a mulch afterwards is the best form of feeding both for quantity and quality. Such dressings contain a little of everything *in balance* and, moreover, help to retain soil moisture so that nutrients can be used to the full. Even if such material is in short supply, it is well worthwhile trying to arrange for occasional supplies. Apply the mulch in spring after the soil has warmed up, and preferably following rain when it is uniformly moist.

Feeding with rotted farmyard manure is an ideal many of us cannot always satisfy. The question of what fertilizers to use, and when, is summarized on pp. 44–7. Used correctly, both artificial fertilizers and others can and do give excellent results. But wherever possible use them to supplement rather than replace whatever manure and compost can be spared for mulching. Specific details for individual crops are mentioned in the chapters concerned.

Mineral Deficiencies

Often through lack of manuring, or even in spite of it, there develops a deficiency of one or other of the plant nutrients essential to healthy growth. In the early stages the trouble may remain insignificant and unnoticed, but as the deficiency becomes more acute the effects show up in the form of unhealthy foliage. This is not diseased foliage, but rather leaves which are not their normal healthy green and which cannot therefore function properly. The interesting thing is that the deficiencies usually take on a well-defined individual pattern in the leaf, from which they can be recognized by the experienced eye. It is a case, however, of a little knowledge being a dangerous thing, and unless one is well versed and quite sure what the trouble is, it is much wiser to seek an expert opinion so that any corrective measures taken may be the right ones.

The likeliest deficiencies to be found in soft fruits are:

(a) NITROGEN. Plants suffering from nitrogen deficiency generally show pale-green weak-looking foliage, and in advanced cases growth is poor or even non-existent, with attendant lack of crop. Any fruit will probably be small and seedy.

Control. The immediate measure should be to apply a quick-acting nitrogenous fertilizer such as sulphate of ammonia (or on acid soils Nitro Chalk or Nitra Shell) at $1\frac{1}{2}$ oz. per sq. yd. This should preferably be applied between February and May, but it is doubtful whether any real harm is done by summer dressings. Apply the fertilizer to moist ground and water it in. Surface dressings of rotted farmyard manure and/or compost are also important.

(b) POTASH. Potash is a very important nutrient. It improves fruit quality and leads to firm, well-ripened shoots and growth which will show good resistance to any pest or disease trouble, as well as to winter cold.

Gooseberries and red currants suffer from a deficiency of potash quicker than most, a grey brown or ashen scorching appearing around the edges of the leaves. In severe cases the whole leaf becomes affected, leading to severe premature defoliation.

Control. Apply sulphate of potash as soon as the trouble appears at 1 to $1\frac{1}{2}$ oz. per sq. yd. Unlike the correction of most other deficiencies, that of potash is slow to take effect. A severe deficiency may take a year or two to rectify. Under normal conditions $\frac{1}{2}$ oz. to the sq. yd of sulphate of potash annually or 1 oz. biennially should prove adequate to maintain normal healthy growth. Winter or early spring is the best time to apply it, although any month is possible, since this fertilizer is quite harmless and is not washed out and wasted as nitrogen can be.

(c) MAGNESIUM. Far too little has been made in the past of the importance of adequate magnesium. Gardeners are frequently reminded of the importance of nitrogen, phosphates and potassium but seldom of magnesium. Magnesium is necessary for the production of strong dark-green shoots; without it foliage will take on certain purplish-brown patterns, starting on the lower, older leaves of a shoot. Just as in the case of severe potash deficiency, such leaves drop prematurely and the bush or plant is much weakened in consequence. All soft fruits are vulnerable to magnesium deficiency, blackcurrants, gooseberries and raspberries particularly so.

Control. In this instance a spray on the leaves is the remedy. Dissolve 1 lb. of magnesium sulphate (Epsom Salt) in 5 gallons of water and add a little wetting agent. Apply the spray to the young foliage soon after the fruit has formed and in bad deficiencies repeat the dose at least once, possibly twice, at fourteen day intervals. Ground dressings of magnesium sulphate at 3 oz per sq. yd can also be given, but any benefit derived therefrom seems to be very slow and insignificant. On very acid soil use magnesian limestone at 4 oz. per sq. yd.

(d) IRON. This is one of those deficiencies that is usually brought about by the presence of too much lime (where the pH reading is higher than 7·0). The other is manganese (see below), and both are collectively referred to as 'lime-induced chlorosis'. With iron deficiency the trouble starts at the tips of the shoots: the leaves become pale yellow to milky white in colour except for the green patterning of the veins, and growth and cropping capacity suffer in consequence. Any crop can suffer the deficiency, but raspberries are quicker than most to show it.

Control. Fortunately there is now a fairly simple, albeit rather costly, remedy available. This takes the form of chelated compounds of iron (sequestrene) which, if watered into the soil thoroughly in early spring, or sprayed onto the foliage in a mixture according to maker's instructions, quickly but temporarily alleviate the trouble. For a longer-lasting effect rake in fritted trace elements. Coupled with this, lime – and fertilizers containing lime (like Nitro Chalk and basic slag) – should be avoided. The humus content should be improved at every opportunity by applying well-rotted dung and compost as a surface mulch (see p. 45). Dressings of sulphate of ammonia to supply nitrogen also help to increase acidity.

(e) MANGANESE. This must not be confused with magnesium. As explained above, manganese deficiency may occur where lime content is high. It can be diagnosed from the yellow patterning of the lower older leaves on shoots (as opposed to the whitening of shoot tips with iron deficiency). Again, the veins stand out as a green network, although few of the small veins show green, as they do in cases of iron deficiency.

Control. This is another example of the value of foliar sprays: manganese deficiency can be dealt with quite effectively by applying manganese sulphate (again, do not confuse with magnesium sulphate) at approximately $\frac{3}{4}$ oz. in $1\frac{1}{2}$ gallons of water. Spray it on as the young growth begins to grow away strongly.

Manures and Fertilizers

Constant reference must be made to numerous manures and fertilizers in any full account of the cultivation of crops. Their use and purpose is second-nature to the professional, but to many more the different names are often very confusing. Briefly, manures and fertilizers can be grouped together as follows:

A. Organic manures, consisting of
   (i) Bulky manures such as farmyard manure, compost and sewage sludge.
   (ii) Non-bulky manures such as bone meal, dried blood and hoof and horn meal.

B. Inorganic fertilizers or 'artificials' e.g. sulphate of ammonia, sulphate of potash and superphosphate.

A. *Organic Manures*

As the name implies, these substances are of animal or vegetable origin. They fall into two convenient categories:

(i) BULKY ORGANIC MANURES. Broadly speaking these include all the bulky animal manures and chicken manure, plus waste products like sewage sludge and mushroom compost. Their great value lies in the fact that they not only contain a little of everything that a plant requires, but they also improve soil structure by adding humus. This means that the soil retains moisture more easily (yet is well drained) and is generally fertile. Time was when one could specify which type of *animal manure* was required, but today one is thankful to get whatever is available. Use it only after it has been stacked for a while and is no longer fresh. Over-fresh animal manures can be very damaging as the ammonia released scorches roots and foliage.

Chicken manure is very potent and should never be applied as one would farmyard manure. If allowed to remain in an unprotected heap it develops into a horrible stodgy mess, is thoroughly obnoxious and, more important, loses a lot of its nutrient value. It should be composted with straw and other vegetable refuse before being used.

Sewage sludge is a material worth considering where manure is difficult to obtain. Many local authorities offer sewage sludge at nominal rates, but the nutrient values vary. Of particular importance is the pH value of the sludge, remembering that figures less than 7·0 indicate acidity, above 7·0 alkalinity (i.e. a distinct lime content). Samples in the last category should be used with care, since repeated applications of sludge with a high lime content can soon lead to deficiencies of iron and manganese (see p. 20).

Mushroom compost is merely the remains of animal manure that has been used on mushroom beds and, as we have seen, it can be of considerable value in the fruit garden. However it frequently contains chalk (easily visible), and in such cases its use should be restricted to acid soils.

Compost from the garden refuse heap is very valuable, though more as a source of humus than as a great reservoir of nutrients.

Just as years of rotting leaves under trees return goodness to the soil, so compost benefits the garden. Every garden should have a compost heap, onto which practically all vegetable waste can be tipped. Weeds (not perennial), lawn mowings,* leaves, kitchen waste, sawdust, straw, poultry manure and so on can all be rotted down in a few months into a nice black friable compost which is invaluable. Things *not* to throw on the heap include paper, sticks and coarse cabbage and bean stalks. Details on making a compost heap will be found in *The Vegetable Garden Displayed* and *The Fruit Garden Displayed*, both published by the R.H.S.

(ii) NON-BULKY ORGANIC MANURES. These are derived from animal and occasionally vegetable remains but, unlike the bulky manures, are processed and are therefore available in bags and packages. They are comparatively expensive, but are without exception extremely valuable sources of nutrients; those of greatest benefit to soft fruits are bone meal and hoof and horn meal. They are particularly useful on poorer, drier soils, as they help to improve fertility generally.

Leading examples include:

Bone meal: Of all fertilizers, bone meal is probably the safest to use, although of itself it cannot be considered a 'be-all and end-all'. It is rich in phosphates and also contains a little nitrogen, the latter being of more particular importance to fruit than the phosphate. These nutrients are only slowly available to plants, however. The usual rate of application is 3 oz. per sq. yd.

Bone flour: Similar to bone meal but contains rather less nitrogen. Use as bone meal.

Fish meal: Since samples of this manure can sometimes be harmful to soft fruits, it is probably safest to avoid it for these crops.

Hoof and horn meal: Finely ground hooves, horns, etc. provide a manure that is rich in nitrogen. Again, its use is invaluable on the lighter, poorer soils and the nitrogen it contains is available over a considerable period to the crop concerned. Various grades of hoof and horn are available; the finer the grist the more quickly available is the nitrogen content. Usual rate of application is 3 oz. per sq. yd.

Soot and wood ash. Soot is a well-known and valuable source

* Not from lawns treated with selective weed killers less than six weeks before.

of nitrogen, but should be weathered for at least three months before use. It can either be scattered like a fertilizer or watered in or be diluted in water and applied as a soot-water soluble feed; use in either case during the spring and early summer. It must not be used in conjunction with lime or roots and foliage may be scorched. Wood ash is a useful source of potash but, like bone meal, an occasional scattering of it does not work the miracles so many seem to think. The amount of potash it contains is quite small, but providing the ash is stored dry until use it can do nothing but good. It is most valuable on heavier ground, where it can help to improve soil structure.

B. *Inorganic Fertilizers (or 'Artificials')*

These are either obtained from natural deposits (e.g. Chilean nitrate of potash) or are products resulting from various chemical processes. Hence the loose but well-known nick-name of 'artificials'. As far as we are concerned the most important fertilizers for use on soft fruits are sulphate of ammonia, Nitro Chalk and Nitra Shell to provide nitrogen; superphosphate and basic slag to supply phosphates; and sulphate of potash for potash.

Sulphate of ammonia: Probably the best known of all quick-acting, nitrogenous fertilizers. It has an acid reaction and because of this its use is advised on limey ground in particular. Average rate of application is 1 oz. per sq. yd.

Nitro Chalk and Nitra Shell are very popular nitrogenous fertilizers among fruit-growers. The granules are easily spread and the free lime content means that these are the fertilizers to use on *acid* soil. On the other hand they should not be used on alkaline ground (to be on the safe side use only where the pH is below 6·0). Usual rate of application is about 1 oz. per sq. yd.

Superphosphate: The most widely used phosphatic fertilizer. Although frequent applications of phosphates do not seem to be necessary for fruit, a little superphosphate is usually advised every few years for most crops. Usual rate of application is 3 oz. per sq. yd.

Sulphate of potash: This is the standard potash fertilizer. It can be used on all crops but excessive dressings should be avoided, as they can lead to magnesium deficiency. Average rate of application is $\frac{1}{2}$–1 oz. per sq. yd.

Muriate of potash: This is not recommended since under certain conditions it can cause scorch damage, particularly to gooseberries, red currants and raspberries.

6 · Strawberries

The two great advantages of strawberries are that they need so little space and give such quick returns. With reasonable soil and healthy plants there is no reason why fine crops of strawberries should not be picked within nine months of planting. No other hardy fruit can match this for speed of fruiting.

Although wild strawberries abound in Britain, the fine cultivars (varieties) we know today have largely resulted from crosses made between two American species introduced into Europe in the eighteenth century, *Fragaria virginiana*, and its variety *illoensis*, from North America, and *Fragaria chiloensis* from Chile. The first two have a small aromatic fruit, while the latter is much larger with a deep-red colouring.

Summer-fruiting Strawberries

In a warm, early season it is quite possible to pick ripe strawberries in the latter half of May, and with the help of cloches two to three weeks earlier still. The introduction of new strawberries is now a deliberate and controlled operation, largely in the hands of the research stations, with the commercial growers' requirements primarily in mind. And although, by virtue of this, his choice of varieties is more limited, the gardener at least has access – though not always easy access – to the same healthy certified stock for gardens as the commercial grower. The chief difficulty sometimes met with is that of finding a source willing to sell small quantities of runners.

In the case of perpetual-fruiting strawberries and, to a lesser extent, alpine strawberries the position is rather different, as will be seen later.

Frost

As it is a small plant, growing only a few inches above soil level, the flowers of the strawberry are unfortunately very prone to frost damage. Since the main flush of blossom occurs in early to mid-

May, there is always a risk of frost damage. The flowers are very susceptible to frost and soon show 'black eyes' when a sharp night has taken its toll. Ways of combating frost are discussed on p. 15, but for the average-sized strawberry bed it should not be difficult to cover at least some of the plants on colder nights. It is surprising what protection sheets of newspaper can give, or straw lightly spread over the plants. The cultivars themselves vary in susceptibility to frost. This seems to hinge primarily on whether or not the trusses of flowers are protected by the foliage.

The use of straw, to cover plants lightly against frost, should not be confused with the cultural practice of strawing-down. The former gives protection from frost; the latter, if done too soon, does exactly the opposite. This cannot be too strongly emphasized – one frequently sees straw spread between the plants far too early. It merely serves to trap warm air underneath. As a result the temperature on cold nights just *above* the straw is markedly colder, since it is not being 'diluted' by warmth from the soil. This causes far greater damage to flowers than would otherwise have occurred.

Site

In general an open sunny site should be chosen. With a little forethought, however, it is surprising how much use can be made of different aspects to prolong the season of fruiting – even without the aid of cloches. A few plants sitting snugly against a warm south-facing wall or fence can be a week or more in advance of the open bed. Then, for late use, a few more plants in a more shaded position will prolong the season. Since we are, or should be, mostly concerned with quality and flavour, however, the sunnier the situation the better.

Soils

The modern-day building practice of bulldozing off topsoil may mean that infertile soil remains, in which case steps should be taken as outlined on p. 19. But most soils will give fair results providing (a) they are prepared correctly and (b) healthy plants are used. Light soils may produce earlier crops but these may not be so heavy or last for so long as those on better loams (and even well-worked clays) which are more retentive of moisture. A medium-light loam is the soil to aim for . . . if it can ever be found!

A word of warning concerning chalk soils. These frequently cause lime-induced chlorosis among strawberries, rendering them short-lived and poor-cropping. Such soils should be given liberal dressings of humus and built up to better fertility (see p. 45). Results will then be much more rewarding. If iron deficiency (see p. 43) does occur, some alleviation of the trouble can be obtained by using sequestrene.

The avoidance of waterlogged or badly drained areas needs no emphasis. Apart from other considerations wet soils encourage red core disease (see p. 70). Lack of water on lighter soils and attendant loss of crop may not, on the other hand, be so obvious. First fruits may form but the remainder quickly fall off in size and many may never develop at all without the aid of timely and copious watering. Indeed, it is not uncommon to see whole plants collapsing through drought.

Preparation of the Bed

Correct preparation of the soil before planting is a key factor to success. If the ground has been well worked and fed, as in a vegetable garden, ordinary single-digging or mechanical cultivation incorporating some farmyard manure or compost will suffice. If it has not, double-digging is preferable to ensure a good depth of ground for the roots to feed on. The vegetable garden lends itself to the inclusion of strawberries. The ground is normally fertile and reasonably clear of weeds, and there is usually a strip available to accommodate an annual planting of a row or two of new runners. Ground recently cleared of potatoes, peas, beans or onions is ideal because it will probably have been manured. (Potatoes, however, increase the incidence of Verticillium disease among strawberries; see p. 70.) Annual weeds can be skimmed off and buried, but pernicious perennials like couch and bindweed are a different proposition. In fact, if there is anything more than a smattering of such weeds no planting should be done until the ground is completely clean.

Prepare the ground some weeks before planting to allow the soil to settle naturally. After digging and before levelling to a planting tilth apply the following fertilizers, if no manure is available:

Bone meal at 3 oz. per sq. yd
Hoof and horn meal at 3 oz. per sq. yd
Sulphate of potash at 1 oz. per sq. yd

9. (*Left*) Strawberry plant ridden with virus disease. (*Right*) A healthy plant. Runners *must* be taken from healthy plants.

The fertilizers are scuffled in during the process of levelling. Ground should be really firm for planting and also moist, so that it should be watered as necessary.

Buying Healthy Plants

As explained in Chapter 3 virus diseases are a menace to soft fruits and to strawberries in particular (Pl. 9). It cannot be too strongly emphasized that for consistently good results it is imperative to plant only healthy certified runners.

A glance at the horticultural press during the summer and early autumn will reveal numerous reliable sources of supply – firms who specialize in the production of runners and whose stock must have been inspected before being offered for sale. There is one snag, however – many of these firms are wholesale only and will not accept small orders. If in doubt the paper containing the advertisement may well be able to offer advice on a likely source for a few runners.

10. Strawberry runners planted 18 ins. apart in rows 3 ft apart. This can be reduced slightly for less vigorous cultivars, but adequate spacing as shown here is essential.

Planting Distances

These will depend on (a) how long the plants are to be kept, (b) soil type and (c) the growth habit of individual cultivars. A standard recommendation used to be $2\frac{1}{2}$ or 3 ft between rows with plants 18 ins. apart in the rows (Pl. 10). However, the size of plant varies considerably from one cultivar to another – 'Red-gauntlet', for instance, requires less space than 'Cambridge Vigour'. Such differences are further influenced by the type of soil involved.

Probably the best approach is to experiment under one's own

conditions. Plant half the bed at, say, 2 ft 6 ins. × 1 ft 6 ins. and the remainder at 2 ft 6 ins. × 1 ft. Experience should soon show which spacing is best and future plantings can be adjusted accordingly. One thing is certain – well-spaced plants will always give better results than overcrowded ones.

Some commercial growers, aiming at early fruit and the high prices paid for it, are now treating strawberries as an annual crop. For this, much closer planting is possible, particularly in the rows – 2 ft 6 ins. × 9 ins. for example. This would be equally acceptable for the garden, but it is doubtful if many gardeners would be persuaded to discard healthy strawberry plants after only one season. Neither is it necessary.

The matted row is an alternative method of growing strawberries. The planting layout is the same as that already described, the difference being in subsequent treatment whereby runners are allowed to form between and adjacent to plants in the row, at the same time keeping a clean alley between rows. This can be highly productive in drier seasons, but such gains may be more than offset by losses through rotting in wet ones. There is also the risk that fruit may be smaller because of the plants being overcrowded.

Planting

Runners planted by early September will give excellent crops of large fruits early the following summer. The earlier they are planted the heavier the crop should be. Even late September and October plantings can give some fruit. Any runners put in after mid-October, or in the spring, however, should be deblossomed. They will then build up into sturdy plants and crop heavily a year later.

Under normal conditions rooted runners are not usually ready in any quantity until late July, or even August in many areas. The bed should be levelled, firmed and marked out so that planting can be done as soon as the runners are received. Using a taut garden line to give a straight row, take out a hole with a trowel. The crown in the centre of the runner should be sitting with its base just at soil level when planting is completed. Too deep and it will be buried, too shallow and roots will be showing. The placing of each plant against the line will make planting much easier, as one's fingers can use the soil surface behind the line as a firm base to keep the plant steady and at the correct depth.

Plant firmly, particularly on lighter soils, and rake over the bed. Watering-in is usually necessary, using either an open-spouted can at each planting site or a fine spray line to water over-all. Later in the autumn as the ground thaws after frost the new plants may easily be half pushed out of the soil, since they will have as yet made insufficient root for permanent anchorage. If this happens each plant should be refirmed carefully without delay.

Mulching and Manuring

Where some well-rotted manure or compost is available it is good practice to apply it as a mulch between the plants to a depth of about 1 in. in early autumn. This is particularly valuable on light sands and gravels, and also on chalky soils.

Basically, however, the all-important part of the manuring programme is the digging-in of plenty of farmyard manure and compost *before planting*. This should enable healthy plants to produce good crops without the aid of fertilizers. The only exception is an annual application of sulphate of potash which is a great help to general health and quality. A dressing of $\frac{1}{2}$ to 1 oz. per sq. yd in late winter will be quite adequate. Nitrogenous fertilizers give no benefit and should not be used.

Weeding

Providing the bed is not invaded by perennial weeds it should not be too difficult to keep it clean. The hoe is most effective when weeds are small and shallow-rooted, and in any case it is much less laborious to tackle seedling weeds than whole tussocks of chickweed, etc., that have probably seeded before one reaches them anyway. Whenever possible choose a dry sunny spell to do the hoeing. Weeds then quickly shrivel up. Use a dutch hoe and do not go too deep or too close to the plants or the roots will be damaged. A draw hoe is not advised because it tends to pull soil away from the plant in one direction and onto it in another. For the use of herbicides to control weeds around strawberry plants see Chapter 15.

Watering

A considerable increase in crop can be obtained by watering at the right time. The crucial period is between flowering and just before picking, that is May–June. Water can be given in dry

11. Strawing-down. This should not be done too early.

12. Polythene mulch laid in position over young strawberry runners (in this instance before cloching). Slits will be made in the polythene and the foliage carefully pulled through.

spells at this time at the equivalent of 1 in. of rainfall; this means a rate of approximately 4½ gallons per sq. yd (for the calculation of this, see p. 23).

It is advisable not to water once the peak of ripening has been reached as this tends to increase grey mould rot (botrytis). Neither is watering before flowering recommended – it tends to induce the formation of too much leaf and this too can increase rotting as well as delaying ripening.

Derunnering

This is always a tiresome but necessary chore in a strawberry bed. A few of the best runners can be left to root but, as explained later and on p. 162, it is preferable to raise runners from a few plants which are isolated from the strawberry bed itself. Runners develop quickly and, like weeds, are much more easily dealt with when young. They are then soft and easy to pinch out; later they can be quite tough and wiry and are then best cut with a knife. Plants will require de-runnering at least twice, possibly three times during the summer.

Strawing-Down

Despite the availability of several proprietary alternatives, straw is still the most widely used material for protecting ripening fruits from the soil and rain splash (Pl. 11). Only a thin layer of straw is necessary and it should not be laid down until all risk of frost is past. This is usually late May, which as it happens just about coincides with the point at which developing fruits are beginning to weigh down the truss, thus requiring protection from the soil. It is again emphasized that too early strawing will considerably increase any damage from frost. Always use clean dry straw; dirty and/or damp samples will only encourage grey mould (botrytis) among the fruit.

Black Polythene 'Mulch'

An inviting alternative to strawing-down is to cover the ground with black polythene the edges of which are buried in the soil to secure the sheeting against wind. Either plant the runners and then carefully pull the foliage through prepared slits in the polythene (Pl. 12), or lay the polythene and then plant through it, having made a slit first. The latter is thought to be preferable. Black polythene of 150 gauge is advised. It is most important to have the soil evenly moist before laying the polythene down. The surface of the bed must be slightly convex, but even, to throw off any rainfall. If it is not, pools of water form and there is an increased risk of trouble from rotting.

Providing the soil is sufficiently moist no watering should be necessary right through till after picking the following year. Results from leaving the polythene undisturbed for a further season are not certain, but it has been found that fruit can become dirty on the lighter soils where soil particles have fallen or blown onto the polythene.

Netting

Netting the bed to protect the crop from birds is essential in the garden. Details about the various kinds of nets, size of mesh, etc., are given in Chapter 1 (p. 11). If grey squirrels are troublesome the only sure way is to have an all-wire netting enclosure or, if only a few plants are being grown, some wire-netting arches over each row. Any risk of drips from the netting doing damage will probably be gladly taken in such circumstances, since a few squirrels can ravage a large bed in a very short time. On the other hand it may be more economic to spend money on shooting the squirrels rather than on wire netting!

Picking

At first only a few fruits will ripen at a time; these will be the biggest, though not always the best flavoured. Pickings quickly increase in weight and plants should be looked over every other day at least, preferably daily in warm weather. Plants normally fruit for 3 to 4 weeks, but hot, dry weather may mean a very short season of two weeks or so.

If possible pick the fruit when it is dry, certainly so if it is intended for jam. A ripe strawberry will not keep for long in uncontrolled conditions, still less if it is picked when wet. Always remove rotting or damaged fruits and bury or burn them; this can help considerably in reducing losses from rotting. Pick the fruit well behind the calyx so that no bruising with the fingers can result and place carefully in a punnet or basin. Fruit for jam can be picked without the stalk or calyx, although it is probably just as quick to remove them in the kitchen later.

The great advantage of garden-grown strawberries over commercial crops is that the fruit can, and indeed should, be left until it is fully and evenly coloured all over – that is, fully ripe. Only at this stage can the true flavour and qualities of a strawberry be appreciated.

Cutting Over and Cleaning

Soon after fruiting has finished, the existing foliage, already tattered, will tend to die off. This is natural prior to the production of fresh young leaves during the late summer. There is experimental evidence to show that the old foliage, if not removed, reduces the amount of flower initiation within the crown for the next year's crop. It is advisable therefore to cut over the plants as soon as fruiting has finished to remove old foliage. A hand sickle can be used, even certain types of grass cutter, no harm coming to the plants providing the foliage is cut at a height of about 4 ins., sufficient to clear the all-important crowns. Most cultivars respond to such treatment by producing rather heavier crops the following year. However, 'Cambridge Favourite' is an exception and should not be cut down.

Coupled with cutting-over is the general cleaning of the bed – all weeds, runners and straw should be cleared away and burnt. This all helps in controlling pests and diseases and keeping plants vigorous and healthy. Where nets are removed it is important to see that they are thoroughly dry and any holes repaired *before* being stored away.

Roguing

At all times during the growing season careful watch should be kept for 'ailing' plants – those that look puny and sickly alongside a normal one. Usually, though not always, the trouble is being caused by one or more of the virus diseases. The quicker such plants are removed and burnt the better, otherwise they may well infect the others.

Cultivars (Varieties)

Although a large number of cultivars are available from one source or another only a select few are grown for the eventual distribution of certified plants. The selection may vary a little from year to year but it is more or less as follows:

A. Cultivars Widely Grown (Certified Stock Usually Available) (*denotes those most highly recommended)

*CAMBRIDGE FAVOURITE. Probably now the most widely grown variety of all. Relatively foolproof, it has a longer season of fruiting than most and is an excellent strawberry for cloche cultivation. Early to mid-season ripening. Rather pale colour fair flavour.

CAMBRIDGE PRIZEWINNER. Increasing in popularity as a first early cultivar. The plant is of a very upright habit, producing conical to wedge-shaped fruits of a brilliant scarlet. Early ripening, short season, rather acid flavour.

*CAMBRIDGE RIVAL. Ideal for those who like a really sweet strawberry, although its very dark colour detracts from its market value. Foliage very erect. Second-early ripening. Of quite good flavour.

*CAMBRIDGE VIGOUR. A very widely grown variety and probably one of the best flavoured. Maiden plants fruit early, older ones nearer to mid-season because of the excessive amount of vigorous foliage. Attractive bright crimson fruit. Good cropper.

MERTON PRINCESS. A very heavy cropper but of inferior flavour and quality. Not recommended for garden purposes. Mid-season.

REDGAUNTLET. These medium-sized fairly open plants produce heavy crops of round, conical or wedge-shaped fruits of a brilliant scarlet colour. Although possessing no great quality or flavour it is less susceptible to botrytis rot than most. Mid to late mid-season, fruit firm and attractive: often produces a useful second crop in early autumn.

*ROYAL SOVEREIGN. Still acknowledged as the best-flavoured strawberry, though it falls far short of most modern varieties in cropping capacity. Very susceptible to virus diseases, mildew and botrytis rot. Early mid-season; the pale scarlet fruit is of excellent quality. Is best grown on its own so that the virus risk is minimized.

*TALISMAN. A strawberry which does well in some areas, not in others, one of the requirements being a good soil. Fruit is attractive and sharply conical, quickly losing size if soil is dry. The plant is very slow to start growth in spring and may even look 'dead' alongside other varieties. Late mid-season; of very good quality and flavour and well worth growing where conditions suit it. A useful second crop is often produced late summer to early autumn.

The following short list includes four new cultivars which may be worthy of trial as they become available.

B. New Cultivars (Varieties) of Promise

GORELLA. A new Dutch strawberry producing large wedge-shaped fruits ripening dark red which show some resistance to botrytis rot. Second early; flavour poor.

MERTON HERALD. Similar in colour to 'Royal Sovereign' but conical in shape with a pronounced neck. Early; of quite good flavour and shows considerable promise as a garden strawberry.

TEMPLAR. A very attractive fruit ripening deep red. Plants are very vigorous. Mid-season; of fair flavour and quality but the very leafy plant results in much grey mould on the fruit in wet weather.

CRUSADER. Quite similar to 'Templar' in habit of plant and appearance and flavour of fruit but second early to mid-season in ripening.

Varieties in the following list are less widely grown but are, for the most part, still available from one or more sources. Not usually available as certified stock.

C. Cultivars Less Widely Grown

AXBRIDGE EARLY. Very early; fair flavour.

CAMBRIDGE ARISTOCRAT. Mid-season; flavour rich and reminiscent of alpine strawberry.

CAMBRIDGE LATE PINE. Late; dark-coloured fruit, sweetly flavoured.

CAMBRIDGE PREMIER. Early; brightly coloured firm fruit, flavour fair.

CAMBRIDGE REARGUARD. Late; soft dark-coloured fruit of indifferent flavour, often acid.

CAMBRIDGE SENTRY. Mid-season; said to do well on heavy soils.

EARLY CAMBRIDGE. Mid-season; of fair flavour only and bruises easily.

HUXLEY. Late mid-season; still widely grown in some areas for jam contracts; being more tolerant of virus diseases than most it acts as a carrier and is not recommended for garden culture.

MADAME LEFEBVRE. Very early; still grown in a few areas; very subject to mildew, botrytis rot and red core and largely superseded.

Perpetual-Fruiting (Remontant or Ever-Bearing) Strawberries

These differ from the well-known and widely grown summer-fruiting kinds in that, although a first flush of fruit may develop in the summer, a second and larger crop is produced during the autumn. In some cases the earliest-formed runners themselves fruit in the autumn along with the parent plant.

The perpetual-fruiting strawberries were developed originally on the continent and more recently in the United States. Apart from a scheme on a limited scale for one cultivar in Scotland there is no certification scheme as yet for them. Because of this the health status of plants is always open to question. Consequently it is well to grow them separately from the summer-fruiting types, which may quickly become infected with any viruses the perpetual types are carrying. Equally, however, many perpetual-fruiting cultivars are themselves virus-sensitive, so that variable results must be expected.

The cultivation of these perpetual-fruiting strawberries is identical to that of summer-fruiting varieties. Thorough preparation, adequate manure and compost to ensure a fertile moisture-holding soil, freedom from perennial weeds and rigorous roguing of sickly plants at first sight – all these are essential. The use of cloches will usually be necessary to pick the later fruits and by so doing it is possible to pick ripe fruit in November, though quality and flavour will naturally have fallen off by then.

Runners are not usually available until the autumn and most authorities advise spring planting. If this is done the young plants are deblossomed until late June so that they can become fully established before cropping. Such deblossoming can be done annually on all plants if desired, since it usually leads to heavier and more prolonged fruiting in late summer and autumn. With spring planting adequate watering would be vital. The annual planting of at least some new runners is advisable providing they are healthy.

Some Cultivars of Perpetual-Fruiting Strawberries

HAMPSHIRE MAID. One of the best remontants; very similar to 'Saint Claude'; a heavy cropper, the fruit is attractive and well flavoured. Vigorous.

RED RICH. Raised in U.S.A.; vigorous heavy-cropping plants; fruit dark red, sweet and fragrant.

SAINT CLAUDE. A well-tried and nicely flavoured strawberry. One of the best remontants.

SANS RIVALE. Probably the best-known remontant. Moderately vigorous, heavy-cropping plants. Fruit brilliant and glossy, with quite good flavour.

TRIOMPHE. Said to be more resistant to virus diseases than many. Orange-scarlet fruits of very good flavour. Does well on most soils.

The 'Climbing' Strawberry

One or two perpetual-fruiting varieties, 'Sonjana' in particular, have been publicized under this misnomer. Certainly the newly formed runners will fruit as claimed but they will *not* climb unless helped to do so by tying them to a convenient trellis or wire netting. 'Sonjana' is a good-flavoured variety, but many who have tried it find that it is outclassed in cropping capacity by most of the other perpetual-fruiting varieties. One reason for this is the susceptibility of 'Sonjana' to virus troubles.

The Alpine Strawberry

The small, very fragrant fruits of the alpine strawberry are highly prized by some people, although a good deal of patience in picking is required! Plants can be bought and nurserymen usually raise them from seed, as no runners are produced; this is more satisfactory than attempting to divide up older plants. A partly shaded border with a leafy, moisture-holding soil is recommended. Some white-and-pink-fruited forms are known, but the leading, indeed the only, cultivar normally listed is 'Baron Solemacher'.

Strawberries under Cloches

Those gardeners who possess a number of cloches will probably already know, to their satisfaction, how valuable they are for producing early strawberries as well as the autumn-fruiting perpetual types (see p. 61). With luck the first fruits from open-ground plants will ripen in early to mid June; those under cloches should be available two to three weeks earlier. The growers barn-type cloche (Pl. 12) is the one most widely advocated

13. Strawberries under tent cloches.

although the simple tent cloche (Pl. 13) can produce very early crops. Polythene sheeting can also be used effectively to form a tent over the plants instead of cloches, a technique now used by many commercial growers.

The time of cloching is important. To cover the plants too early is a mistake, because a sudden warm spell may induce rapid growth which can be severely checked by ensuing cold. The best time over most of southern England and Wales is probably late February, delaying the date for one or two weeks in colder northern and eastern areas, or advancing it by a week or two in particularly favoured areas such as the south-west and extreme south.

The watering of plants under cloches may prove necessary in drier seasons, but the reservoir of moisture on better garden soils should reduce this to a minimum. The effective watering of a large area of cloched strawberries presents problems, but for the few plants normally involved in garden culture it is quite easy. The judicious application of one or two cans of water or the use of a trickling hose is usually sufficient. But whatever the method the water must be applied without splashing the fruit.

Some straw spread along outside the cloches will help as a mulch in conserving soil moisture. Straw is not normally necessary inside the cloche, however, since the glass prevents any splashing of the fruit. The drier conditions inside the cloche do in fact greatly reduce the percentage loss of fruit from botrytis rot (grey mould) and in wet seasons the use of cloches on strawberries over as long a period as possible will certainly save many fruits.

Barn cloches are usually adjustable for ventilation. This will not usually be necessary until a really warm spell develops, and in very hot weather light shading may be called for. Tent cloches have to be moved an inch or so apart to facilitate adequate ventilation.

Under normal garden practice runners are planted at the usual spacing (see p. 52) and the required number cloched in February. If for a particular reason the plants are to remain for one season only, then planting distances should be reduced to 8–10 ins. with perhaps a double row under the larger barn cloche, the rows 10-15 ins. apart. Some favour the double row, others not, depending to a considerable extent on particular soils and conditions and also cultivar.

For garden purposes cloches are an asset on all cultivars. Some profit from them more than others, however, the less leafy ones being the favourites, since the extra light means earlier ripening. If you are planting with a cloched crop particularly in mind, the following cultivars would be a good choice: 'Cambridge Vigour', 'Cambridge Favourite', 'Cambridge Prizewinner', 'Cambridge Rival' and 'Royal Sovereign'.

Strawberries in Glasshouses

The forcing of strawberries in glasshouses requires some heating, otherwise there is no worthwhile gain over cloched plants. Like all pot-grown crops, strawberries grown in this way need precise and regular attention and unless this can be given the project is not worth pursuing. With heat, ripe strawberries should be available from mid-April.

The first step is to root outside strong, healthy runners in 3-in. pots of John Innes Potting Compost No. 1 as early as possible. These must not become root-bound before being repotted into 6-in. pots of J.I.P. Compost No. 3. The plants are then grown on in the open until late November. By then, fully dormant, they should be turned onto their sides in their pots against a wall or fence until brought under glass. Alternatively, they can be housed in a cold frame, in which case maximum ventilation must be allowed, the main purpose being to keep off excessive rainfall.

At the end of December or early January the pots are placed inside on a shelf as close to the glass as practicable. At first no heat is necessary, but once new leaves show, a minimum night temperature of 45°F. is required, increasing to 50°F. during the day. As the flower trusses begin to show the night temperature should be raised to 50°F. and that during the day to 55-60°F. A further increase of 5 to 10 degrees is necessary during flowering and until ripening starts. It is then important to drop the temperature a little, as this enhances flavour.

Correct ventilation is important. It should be given only when the recommended day-time temperature for each stage has been reached. Draughts must be avoided. Equally essential is correct watering. The need will be negligible until growth commences, but it should be gradually and then rapidly increased as the crop develops. In the late stages, particularly during ripening, the plants will require checking for water two or three times daily.

The maintenance of a moist atmosphere is necessary, otherwise red spider mite may prove troublesome. However, when plants are in full flower, drier conditions are desirable to assist pollination.

Pollination with a rabbit's tail or fine brush is advisable to reduce the possibility of poorly shaped fruits. Fruit size and quality is improved if the smaller, later flowers are pinched off and the crop per plant restricted to not more than ten fruits.

In the writer's opinion, however, a forced strawberry is but a pale shadow of its summer counterpart and probably is not worth the time and detailed work involved under normal circumstances.

Pests

There are a few pests that are a regular threat to strawberry-growing and considerably more that may prove troublesome at times. The commonest are:

APHIDS (greenfly). A number of different aphids may be found on strawberries. The most serious is the strawberry aphid, because it is the chief carrier of virus diseases, although any physical damage it may cause on its own account is negligible. It is creamy white in colour. The shallot aphid, on the other hand, is pale greenish-brown and can cause serious curling of the foliage, usually in April–May following a mild winter.

Control. Spray with dimethoate or malathion before flowering and again after fruiting. Alternatively, use sprays of nicotine or derris, or runners should be dipped in or sprayed with malathion when planting.

BIRDS. The necessity of netting a strawberry crop against birds is obvious. Linnets can cause unusual, superficial damage by pecking the seeds off the surface of the fruit.

SLUGS AND SNAILS. Most troublesome on the heavier, wetter soils where damage can be very serious. Strawing-down too thickly will accentuate the trouble.

Control. By using one of the numerous proprietary slug baits and other formulations based on metaldehyde.

Other pests that may be encountered include:

CATERPILLARS. Occasionally caterpillars, particularly the tortrix, can be troublesome.

Control. Derris spray or dust; DDT spray if not a danger to ripening fruit.

EELWORMS. It is extremely difficult for the gardener to take any effective action against any of these pests, most of which are microscopic in size. Moreover it is unlikely that amateur growers would be aware of the presence of eelworms, the adverse effects of which would probably be attributed to 'the season' or 'the soil'. The leaf-and-bud eelworms, as well as the stem-and-bulb eelworms, cause malformation of the leaves and crowns of strawberry plants. Another group, the free-living eelworms in the soil, are responsible for the spread of the virus disease, arabis mosaic.

Control. Any control measures that are available to commercial growers (e.g. hot-water treatment of runners for fifteen minutes in water at 115°F. for both leaf-and-bud and stem-and-bulb eelworms) are extremely difficult if not impossible for gardeners to carry out. Also if soil eelworm is shown to be causing arabis mosaic virus disease there is no answer other than not growing strawberries on the ground concerned. There are good grounds for suspicion where it is certain that runners were healthy to start with and that soil structure and nutrients and other standard cultural requirements are not suspect. In such instances expert advice should be sought.

MICE. Mice can be very troublesome if waste ground, hedges or similar cover surround the strawberry bed. Many fruits may be spoilt, rendering the whole crop distasteful.

Control. Trapping and the use of a suitably protected vermin bait. The clearing of long grass, etc., in the vicinity of the strawberry plants will also help.

MOLES. These can be particularly harmful to newly planted runners. The organic dressings incorporated in preparing the bed encourage a large earthworm population which in turn attracts moles.

Control. The best method is trapping, providing a main 'run' can be found. This may not be on the bed itself, but it is worth the effort to find one – it will usually remain a good trapping site year after year.

RED SPIDER MITE. Heavy infestations can build up in suitably warm conditions, particularly under cloches. Yellowish-brown mottling appears on the foliage; the scarcely visible mites feed by sucking sap from the underside of leaves and have a generally weakening effect.

Control. If dimethoate or malathion is used regularly pre-blossom against aphids it should also take care of red spider in most seasons. Alternatively, use derris, although several applications will be necessary.

SEED BEETLES. Browsing on the seeds on the fruits' surface, these pests can cause substantial losses. However, it is now realized that much of the damage at one time attributed to seed beetles is in fact caused by linnets, which carefully peck the seeds from the fruit. Seed beetles are usually found in rough grass or weeds adjacent to the strawberries.

Control. By cultivation of surrounding area and keeping grass cut short.

Soil Pests

These include wireworms and the grubs of chafers, strawberry root weevil and vine weevil and swift moth. Occasionally they may damage the roots of strawberry plants, which in severe cases may collapse.

Control. Although there are certain chemicals that can be applied to the soil this is not a desirable procedure for garden soft fruits. Since grass and weedy ground encourage such pests clean gardening is essential for control. Serious trouble is seldom experienced except possibly for the first year on newly broken pastureland. Leaving the ground roughly cultivated for the winter will expose many of the grubs and wireworms to birds.

SQUIRRELS. The grey squirrel is a menace to a ripening strawberry crop in some areas. Whole fruits are eaten and many more torn from the plants and spoilt.

Control. Grey squirrels are so destructive that their numbers should be reduced wherever practicable either by direct shooting, or trapping and then shooting. Crops should be protected by wire netting where possible; nylon or fish netting is useless as squirrels will gnaw through.

STRAWBERRY MITE (Tarsonemid Mite). This can be a troublesome pest in southern England in warm summers. The tiny mites cause the young leaves to become crinkled, thus seriously disrupting growth. Plants may appear dwarfed, as though stricken with some virus disease.

Control. The pest is not widespread. This is fortunate, because there is no practical control on a garden scale. Commercial growers use hot-water treatment, 115°F. for seven minutes.

WIREWORM. See Soil Pests, above.

Diseases (Other than Virus)

Two are particularly common, namely botrytis and mildew, and regular, routine spraying is advised against both.

BOTRYTIS (Grey Mould). Often erroneously referred to as mildew because of the mouldy fruits (Pl. 14). Is particularly severe in moist humid conditions and causes heavy losses of fruit.

Control. Wider spacing of plants to allow more airy conditions and coupled with this the control of weeds. Removal of any fruit that is showing rotting. Spraying with dichlofluanid, as

14. Grey mould (botrytis) on strawberries.

specified by the makers, gives a good control. Dichlofluanid also has the advantage of not tainting preserved samples of fruit.

Alternatively spray with thiram or captan as flowers begin to open and repeat twice at ten-day intervals, including full bloom. Thiram is more effective than captan. Later applications should be avoided on fruit intended for bottling or jamming lest they cause taint and discoloration. The cultivar 'Redgauntlet' is less susceptible to botrytis than most.

MILDEW. Worse on some varieties than others, particularly on 'Royal Sovereign', and most likely to occur in drier years. Mildew is easily distinguished from Botrytis, since it appears mainly on the foliage. Severe attacks can weaken the plants seriously, the mildew eventually spreading from foliage to fruit as well as to the runners. Infected leaves begin to roll upwards and in bad infections become completely covered with mildew and waste away.

Control. Regular applications of dinocap, commencing just before flowering. If the new material dichlofluanid is used for botrytis, mildew often becomes less troublesome as well.

A number of other diseases can occur:

LEAF SPOT. Quite commonly seen, the greyish-red spots can have a weakening effect in serious outbreaks, when the spots coalesce and leaves may wither and disintegrate. Usually, however, symptoms are only slight and do not affect the crop materially.

Control. Pick off and burn more seriously marked leaves. Early infections in particular may need to be controlled to prevent the trouble spreading and plants should be sprayed with Bordeaux mixture. Do not use infected runners.

RED CORE. May be serious in some areas, particularly where drainage is poor. It is spread by using infected runners. The trouble usually occurs in small patches, the plants remaining stunted and sickly in appearance. The infected area will gradually increase, the plants soon dying. When slit open, the centre or core of the root is red, hence 'red core'.

Control. The disease organism can live in the soil for as much as thirteen years. Thus, infected ground must not be used for strawberries. No cure is known, but cultivars resistant to the trouble (e.g. 'Talisman', 'Templar', 'Crusader', 'Cambridge Rival' and 'Cambridge Vigour', and to a lesser extent 'Redgauntlet' and 'Cambridge Prizewinner') and raised under the Ministry certification scheme should minimize any chance of an outbreak. This is a serious disease and expert advice should be sought if it is suspected.

VERTICILLIUM. Like red core, this disease is soil-borne. Whole plants may quickly wilt for no apparent reason. Such specimens are usually scattered rather than in patches and recovery is unlikely.

Control. Again, no curative measures are possible. Affected specimens must be burnt and the ground used for other crops. 'Cambridge Vigour' is particularly susceptible and to a lesser extent 'Cambridge Rival'.

Virus Diseases

The vital importance of these has already been underlined earlier in this chapter and in Chapter 3 (Pl. 9). The whole subject is a complex one, particularly as cultivars vary in their susceptibility to them. The effects from one virus are not always visible, depending on the cultivar, but a combination of two or more viruses or virus strains may cause a plant to deteriorate. The trouble then spreads to all parts of such a plant, including its runners.

Major viruses affecting strawberries include:

SEVERE CRINKLE. Pale spots on young leaves herald the trouble. The affected parts do not grow with the surrounding areas, so that a crinkled, puckered leaf is formed. 'Royal Sovereign' is particularly susceptible, whereas 'Huxley', although infected, usually shows no symptoms.

YELLOW EDGE. Again, 'Royal Sovereign' is particularly sensitive and 'Huxley' tolerant. Young leaves show a yellowing at the edges, at first vague but becoming rather more marked with a general shortening of the leaf stalk. Symptoms are most marked during the latter half of the summer and early autumn when infected plants have a definite dwarf, flattened appearance.

GREEN PETAL. Young leaves are sometimes small and yellowed and in some cultivars flowers are malformed with small green petals. Deterioration of plants is usually rapid, some dying before the end of the season. The vector of the virus in this instance is not aphids but a leafhopper which spreads the trouble chiefly from clover.

Soil-borne Viruses

The most likely is arabis mosaic. This causes a general mottling and distortion of foliage while plants of 'Cambridge Favourite' and 'Royal Sovereign' are markedly stunted by it. Soil-borne viruses are spread by free-living eelworms (see p. 66).

There is no cure for any of these virus troubles. The only way to deal with them is by prevention, so make sure that you

1. Purchase certified runners.
2. Spray before flowering and after fruiting annually against aphids.
3. Keep adjacent ground clear of weeds and grass.
4. Dig up and burn all affected plants. This is a wise precaution for any strawberry plant that looks unhealthy, particularly if growth is dwarf and stunted.

7 · Raspberries

Raspberries can be grown without much difficulty in most areas of the British Isles – the wild raspberry species, *Rubus idaeus*, from which present-day cultivars have largely been bred, is in fact a woodland plant here. Scotland in particular excels in its production of this fruit and for many years now the acreage of commercial plantations there has exceeded that south of the border. The coolness and generally moist soil conditions of Scotland can produce much more vigorous growth than the southern counties, with a consequent increase in the yield of fruit.

There are two points in particular that make raspberries an invaluable garden crop. Firstly they are one of the quickest fruits to start cropping after planting, beaten into second place only by strawberries: raspberry canes should carry a useful amount of fruit eighteen months after planting (it is a mistake to allow them to crop in their first season, as will be seen later). Secondly, since the raspberry flowers later than most fruits it is much less likely to suffer frost damage. Thus, given healthy plants, there is a very good chance of obtaining good, regular crops of fine fruit from a small area.

Summer-fruiting Raspberries

It is the summer-fruiting cultivars that attract most attention, although interest in certain autumn-fruiting varieties is at the moment increasing. The different pruning treatments required for the two types seem to confuse many people but, as will be seen, there is nothing complicated about either.

Many of the best old cultivars such as 'Pyne's Royal' and 'Red Cross' have to all intents and purposes been lost to cultivation because of virus spread and because at the time no official scheme existed for the controlled propagation of healthy stock. Now, however, such schemes are well established and in consequence the availability of the more popular cultivars is reasonably well assured, except that small quantities of canes may prove difficult to obtain.

Site

The frost risk is not in general as great with raspberries as it is with most other hardy fruits. In fact only the blackberry and loganberry flower later. Nevertheless it is easy to lose sight of the fact that frosts can and do occur in northern districts well into June; for the southern half of the country a frosted crop of raspberry flowers is a rarity.

Two things stand out as a greater risk to raspberries than frost is likely to be, namely waterlogged soil and wind. A succession of dry winters can lead one into a false sense of security. The winters of 1960–61 and 1965–6, for example, were particularly wet and losses were considerable. Although the raspberry likes a cool moist root run it will not stand excessive wetness – the roots are literally suffocated and the plant quickly dies. Therefore, where a garden is liable to flooding in wet winters trouble must be expected if drainage cannot be improved.

The problem of wind damage is particularly irritating because it usually happens just as the crop begins to ripen. The fruiting shoots or laterals that grow out from the previous year's canes become so heavily laden that they pull away at the 'heel' – i.e. where they join the cane. This usually occurs just after picking has started and although broken laterals may not die completely their supply of nutrient-bearing sap is so severely curtailed that remaining fruits often shrivel. Developing young canes can also be severely bruised, sometimes even snapped off at ground level in windy weather and it is always wise to loop the canes in loosely with soft string to reduce such damage.

Raspberries will succeed quite well in partial shade – they are basically a woodland plant, as already mentioned. In a small garden therefore it is quite all right to relegate them to a shaded corner, though an open sunny situation is always to be preferred.

Soil

Once again well-drained loamy soil is the ideal. Shallow sands and gravels can give surprisingly good results with sufficient watering and feeding, particularly mulching, but as this is beyond the scope of many the limitations of such soils especially in periods of drought must be accepted. Heavier loams and clays are excellent, providing there is no risk of waterlogging. Chalky soils pose a problem as always. In general they lack humus, but providing enough rotted manure, peat and compost is given they can and often do produce good crops. Nevertheless, the chalk still has to be contended with and, as raspberries prefer slightly acid conditions to alkaline ones, trouble is common in such circumstances. Iron deficiency in particular is likely to show in the form of pale, almost white, young foliage, while shortage of manganese may also occur (see p. 44). The secret of success in the long run is adequate humus and adequate moisture with good drainage.

Preparing the Ground

The raspberry is a comparatively long-lived plant and there is no way, after planting, of incorporating manure and compost *into* the soil. Excellent though surface mulches are, they cannot offset completely any basic shortage of humus. Moreover, the soil adjacent to a raspberry row soon becomes a mass of roots and it is bad practice to dig in manure because any advantage this might bring is more than offset by root damage. This illustrates just how important thorough preparation of the ground can be; in fact, this is a key factor with most soft fruits.

Obviously, the poorer soils will need the heavier dressings, but all ground will benefit from generous amounts of well-rotted farmyard manure (Pl. 15). This is the best ingredient if it can be obtained, but the usual alternatives of garden compost, peat and leafmould are all well worth using. Mushroom compost and sewage sludge are also possible for very acid soils, but their likely content of lime must be taken into consideration. Whatever dressing is used it should be worked well into the ground and the preparation completed well in advance of the expected planting date. Since autumn is the best planting time, August or September would not be too soon. If manure is scarce rake in bone meal at 3–4 oz. per sq. yd two weeks before planting.

Before any digging is started, however, there are two important requirements to be satisfied. Firstly, the ground must be clean. Annual weeds like groundsel and meadow grass are not a great problem, but pernicious perennial menaces like creeping thistle, bindweed and couch grass must be completely removed. If any of these develop among raspberries they will be difficult, if not impossible, to eradicate.

Secondly, young plants will often not thrive on ground recently vacated by raspberries, blackberries or hybrid berries. It may be

15. Preparing a new planting site for raspberries. The trench, 2–3 ft wide, should have plenty of rotted manure and compost incorporated before the soil is replaced.

easier said than done to find an alternative piece of ground in the garden, but whenever it can be arranged it should be. Apart from other factors, certain virus diseases of the raspberry are soil-borne (by small eelworms) so that the old raspberry patch may be carrying this sort of trouble for any young canes that may be planted there. If another site is out of the question then it will pay to change as many barrows of soil as can be managed before replanting. The job is best done by taking out a trench and incorporating the necessary manure as the soil is changed (Pl. 15).

Bearing in mind that wetness can soon injure raspberries a slightly raised bed is always a good idea for heavier soils. This again is something that can only be arranged *before* planting.

Support

Once the ground has been prepared suitable posts and wire supports must be erected. It is usually best to wait until the soil has settled before tackling this job. If wooden posts are being used, soak the lower half in a solution of copper sulphate (2 lb. copper sulphate in 10 gallons of water) for two or three days; this will extend their life considerably. The best wood to use is peeled chestnut.

There are many systems of support. Posts need to be at least 5 ft high when in position and about 15 ft apart. One of the most straightforward methods is to have two, even three, strands of galvanized wire (20 gauge) nailed to the posts at, say, 18 ins, 3 ft and 4 ft 6 ins. This takes care of short as well as long canes, all of which can be adequately secured. Use new wire as rust can cause scorch damage to canes and foliage. If the row is a long one, end posts will need to be suitably anchored or buttressed to prevent inward splay. It is surprising how even the sturdiest and deepest-sunk post can be pulled inwards during the summer months when the weight of foliage and fruit is considerable, particularly in windy situations.

Where time is strictly limited a cruder form of support can be used. This usually means inserting sufficient posts along the row to carry struts and parallel strands of galvanized wire at about 2–3 ft. The wires on either side of the canes prevent their being bent to the ground and within the wires the canes tend to support each other (Pl. 16). As young canes develop they are simply kept inside the wires. Time-saving though the method is, it is conducive to disease troubles and wind damage and tied-in canes are always preferable.

The Importance of Healthy Canes

Where any doubt exists about the health of raspberry canes, it is unwise to accept them from friends or neighbours, much the better course being to take advantage of the Ministry of Agriculture certification scheme. This works in a similar way to that for strawberries, and stocks of certified raspberry canes are advertised well in advance of the planting season. Orders received are then delivered as soon as certification procedure has been completed in the autumn, but as mentioned earlier it is often difficult to find a source willing to supply small orders. Some do exist, however.

16. Supporting raspberry canes. A simple method with parallel wires. The canes are not tied.

Having stressed the value of obtaining certified virus-free canes it must be understood that such canes are just as liable to become infected by virus as any others. The fact that they have been raised in isolated, controlled conditions does not make them any less susceptible to viruses. Old virus-ridden raspberries must be dug up and burnt *before* any certified canes are bought. If neighbouring gardens harbour similar trouble tact should be used to persuade the owners to follow a similar course. If such measures were taken seriously many more rows of good raspberries would be seen. The spread of certain virus diseases (particularly mosaic) is caused by aphids, the control of which is described on p. 87.

Planting

Autumn, from late October onwards, is the ideal planting time for raspberries. They break into growth very early in the season,

17. Raspberry canes being planted. The small planting trench is sited in the centre of the prepared strip shown in Pl. 15, p. 75.

and this, together with the fact that young canes may possess few roots, means that the earlier planting can be done the better. Late-winter to early-spring planting may run the distinct risk of a check from cold winds and drought unless there is time and labour sufficient to give the extra watering, etc., that is usually required.

Plant firmly with the root system about 3 ins. deep at an average planting distance of 18 ins. (Pl. 17). If a cultivar is being grown that is not too free in cane production (e.g. 'Lloyd George' and 'Malling Jewel') two canes may be planted per hole. The distance between rows should be 6 ft. Should severe frost occur it is most important to refirm the newly planted canes afterwards. The system of planting is a simple one: either the canes can be planted with a spade against a suitably anchored garden line, or the row position can be nicked out against a line with a spade, the line itself then being removed.

If soil conditions are doubtful, particularly if it is too wet, the canes should be heeled in elsewhere until a proper planting tilth can be obtained.

Pruning after Planting

Newly planted canes should be pruned back to 10–12 ins. from the ground soon afterwards, cutting to just above a suitably placed bud. It is a mistake to leave the canes unpruned in the expectation of a crop of fruit the first summer after planting. I have already mentioned the small root system of a freshly planted cane and it is too much to expect this (a) to produce strong new canes and (b) to support any fruit that may develop on the one existing cane that was planted. It is far better to concentrate on quick establishment of the row, and this is aided considerably by pruning. More and stronger new canes should result and these will carry quite a useful crop the *second* summer after planting. By the third season heavy crops can frequently be expected.

Mulching

The value of mulching raspberry canes with rotted manure and compost has been shown repeatedly in numerous trials and experiments and cannot be over-emphasized. A mulch is particularly essential in the spring after planting; it conserves moisture and in keeping the soil cool encourages quick rooting with a consequent increase in strength of cane growth.

It is a mistake to mulch too early on a cold soil (the soil takes longer to warm up) so that some time in mid–late April is probably best. Apply the mulch onto a moist soil; if conditions are dry, irrigate first. By this time the young canes will be well above ground and the mulching material must be applied carefully. Autumn mulching is an alternative, but much of the dressing will have decayed by the following season and soil moisture may not be conserved so efficiently as a result.

Tying-in

As the new canes develop loop them in temporarily, but by August the full complement of fully grown canes will be available and these can then be more permanently secured, once pruning

18. Raspberries tied with a continuous string looped from one cane to the next. Those shown have not slipped in spite of winter gales.

has been completed (see p. 83). Soft string or fillis is satisfactory and a continuous method of stringing is preferable to individual ties. For continuous stringing first secure an end of string to the post. Holding the first cane in its correct position, loop the ball of string around it, then pass it up and over the wire, down past the cane and on to the next one (Pl. 18). With each cane tied to each wire in this way no amount of wind can move them. If tied individually on the other hand, they easily slip along the wires and 'bunch' together. The canes should be spaced 3 to 4 ins. apart.

Tipping

This is done annually at the end of February. Each cane is cut back to a bud 6 ins. above the top wire; shorter canes should have their top 3 to 4 ins. removed. The purpose of such treatment is two-fold. Firstly, it eliminates any diseased cane tips and any that may have been damaged by weather. Raspberry canes are generally hardy, although occasionally they may be damaged by severe winter frosts in low-lying hollows ('Norfolk Giant' is particularly susceptible). Secondly, tip-pruning is said to encourage fruiting by inducing laterals to form over a longer length of cane.

Netting

Some form of protection for the ripening crop is invariably necessary if birds are not to spoil it. Not only is the crop reduced by actual loss of fruit; in feeding the birds naturally perch on laterals, many of which are snapped in the process. Undoubtedly the easiest form of protection is a series of wire or galvanized piping 'hoops' over which a net can be slung very easily (Pl. 19). If cordon fruit trees are being grown the same hoops can be used for a similar purpose later in the season, as well as during the winter to protect the buds.

Picking the Fruit

Raspberries are normally picked by removing the fleshy part of the fruit only. This leaves the white core, or 'hull', of the fruit behind, still attached to the stalk on the cane. Only if fruits are being selected for show purposes should they be picked complete with stalk. Very large fruits may also be picked in this way for dessert if desired.

It is a good rule to pick any fruit when the crop is dry and in no case is this more important than for raspberries. Mould can spoil a sample within three or four hours of picking if the season is wet and the fruit is very soft.

Bearing in mind how easily fruiting laterals can snap off it is best to support them with one hand while picking with the other. The fruit can be very crumbly, some varieties being worse than others, so that it's wiser to pick into a number of small $\frac{1}{4}$-lb. or $\frac{1}{2}$-lb. punnets rather than a large basket. Frequency of picking will depend to some extent on the weather and the area, but, in general, good quantities of fruit can be gathered every other day over a period of two to three weeks. First pickings in favoured southern areas usually come towards the end of June, rather earlier in the sunnier years.

Pruning

No pruning is required at the end of the first summer following planting, although it is advisable to remove any weak canes. The base of the cane that was planted should also be removed, if it has not already been cut out earlier in the summer.

19. A convenient method of netting raspberries.

20. Pruning summer-fruiting raspberries. Old canes are cut out completely and the best new canes tied in 3–4 ins. apart.

From the second summer onwards considerable annual pruning will be necessary (Pl. 20). If the plants are healthy and vigorous more canes than are required will usually be produced. Ideally, a selection should be made when the canes are still only half grown, for even at this stage the stronger ones are already obvious. The early removal of weaker, damaged or superfluous canes will give the remainder more room in which to develop and will possibly reduce disease troubles by improving air circulation. A maximum of five or six canes from each stool (i.e. the clump that develops over the years from the original cane that was planted) should be quite enough.

With picking usually completed in late July to early August, pruning should be done as soon after this as practicable (Pl. 20). The operation is an easy one and simply involves the complete removal of all the old canes that have fruited, cutting them off just above ground level. The best new canes are then tied in as described on p. 79.

Manuring

An annual mulch of rotted farmyard manure or compost in April is the best form of manuring. Where a suitable mulch is in short supply fertilizers should be used. Nitrogen and potash are particularly important; to supply nitrogen use either hoof and horn meal at 3–4 oz. per sq. yd or sulphate of ammonia at 1–$1\frac{1}{2}$ oz. per sq. yd. A good alternative for distinctly acid soils is Nitro Chalk, also at 1–$1\frac{1}{2}$ oz. per sq. yd. To supply potash give an annual dressing of sulphate of potash at $\frac{3}{4}$ oz. per sq. yd, but if a soil is known to be high in potash such a dressing should be necessary in alternate years only. Every second or third year some phosphates should also be included, giving either bone meal or super phosphate at 3 oz. per sq. yd. All the fertilizers are best spread in February to early March. If a general fertilizer is used choose one high in nitrogen and potash.

Mention has already been made of the raspberry's dislike of an excess of lime and the desirability of having a soil pH of around 6.0. Alkaline soils (above pH 7.0) usually cause deficiency troubles either of iron or of manganese, perhaps both. In each case foliage becomes pale (chlorotic): from the tip downwards where iron is lacking and on older, lower leaves in the case of manganese deficiency. An additional symptom of iron deficiency is that the leaf veins remain green.

To overcome these troubles is not easy unless the soil itself can be improved by rapidly building up its humus content with manure and compost mulches. Rooting is thus encouraged in the surface layer of humus so formed and this helps to offset any ill-effects from the alkaline soil underneath. The use of sequestrene is a distinct possibility but it will need applying annually unless and until the soil is improved. Lawn mowings are often used as a mulch, but those from lawns recently treated with selective weed-killers must be avoided for at least six weeks. These are suitable in small quantities, but on no account should they be put on thickly because they may heat up and encourage disease at the base of the canes. They also tend to mat together and so prevent easy access for rain to the soil beneath.

Roguing

Where growth is poor, expert advice should be sought if the reason is not known. A row of raspberries should certainly last eight years, frequently longer, before old age takes its toll. The ill-effects of virus diseases (Pl. 22, p. 91) are often slower in appearing than with strawberries, and cropping may deteriorate slowly over a year or two rather than falling off rapidly.

Providing soil conditions are suitable any dwarfing of canes may well be caused through virus, in which case the digging-up and burning of stools thus affected is the only sensible solution.

Watering

Raspberries must have a cool *moist* soil to crop well. Mulching and thorough preparation of the bed will do much to meet this, but in drier years watering will be necessary to maintain cropping. Without it many of the later fruits will shrivel and the season of fruiting will be quite short. Moreover, the growth of young canes will also suffer. Indeed, it has been proved experimentally that watering, even in years of adequate rainfall, invariably increases the crop.

An open-ended or perforated hose laid along the row (each side in turn) is the best method of watering, moving it from time to time to ensure a thorough soaking. A minimum of $4\frac{1}{2}$ gallons per sq. yd is advised, the equivalent to 1 in. of rain (for calculation of this see p. 23). Indiscriminate overhead sprinkling tends to increase mouldy fruits and the soil may not be penetrated sufficiently to make it of much advantage.

Cultivars

The list from which to make one's choice is small, and all except 'Lloyd George' and 'Norfolk Giant' have been introduced since the Second World War. The leading cultivars, in approximate order of ripening, are:

MALLING PROMISE. This ripens early and has good quality and flavour. It is very vigorous and heavy-cropping, and like 'Malling Exploit' (below) presents the problems of suckering well away from the row, and producing branched canes. It suffers from botrytis on the fruit in wet weather, but is fairly tolerant of virus troubles.

MALLING EXPLOIT. This ripens early and is very similar in all respects to 'Malling Promise'. The fruit is large or very large but may be crumbly.

LLOYD GEORGE. Like the strawberry 'Royal Sovereign', raspberry 'Lloyd George' came near to extinction because of virus troubles. Thanks to a clean stock from New Zealand, however, this raspberry is still available. A healthy stock should produce strong canes that crop heavily. Unfortunately, it seldom performs in this way and results are frequently disappointing owing to fairly rapid degeneration through virus infection.

Where it can be grown successfully 'Lloyd George' is still considered the best-flavoured raspberry. Its period of ripening is considerably longer than most and the fruits colour early. Useful autumn crops are also produced at the tips of young canes and if necessary this cultivar can be grown specifically for autumn cropping (see p. 86). It makes excellent jam.

MALLING JEWEL. Probably the most widely grown raspberry now and especially popular in Scotland. In the south cane numbers may be disappointing if conditions do not suit their production but 'Malling Jewel' is so good in other respects that it is always worth a trial because of its fine quality and flavour. Fruiting is early to mid-season; crops can be heavy and fruiting laterals are compact and less liable to wind damage than many. Botrytis is less of a problem than on cultivars like 'Malling Exploit' and 'Malling Promise' because the canes and foliage are less dense. Not particularly prone to virus troubles.

MALLING ENTERPRISE. A very useful raspberry since it bridges the gap in cropping between the early cultivars like 'Malling Promise' and the late 'Norfolk Giant'. It crops well where canes are numerous enough and has a good flavour. The fruits are large, maintain their size and make excellent jam.

NORFOLK GIANT. This cultivar is still prized for its late ripening which is some three to four weeks later than the early raspberries. It is rather acid for dessert. It probably suffers more than other raspberries from severe winter weather, so preferably avoid it for low-lying areas renowned for frost. Its susceptibility to virus and indeed its performance generally is variable, but where it can be grown it is well worth trying. The fruit is only medium in size, more purplish-red in colour than most other raspberries, and also more acid. Particularly good for jamming and bottling.

YELLOW-FRUITED CULTIVARS. Occasionally yellow-fruited raspberries are listed. These may well be equal in flavour to red-fruited forms but none of them is available as certified stock. Their cultivation is identical to that for the red cultivars.

Autumn-fruiting Raspberries

Although far less popular than their summer counterparts, the autumn-fruiting raspberries are in constant, if limited, demand. It is possible that interest in them will increase if and when virus-free cultivars are made available. Their cultivation is the same as that for the summer cultivars with one important exception. This is the method of pruning. As mentioned on page 85 autumn fruit is produced on the young canes that developed *during* the summer. These are left unpruned during the winter (the last fruits being picked late October–November) and *all are then cut down to ground level* at the end of February annually.

'SEPTEMBER.' This American introduction is the best at present. Canes are comparatively short but are erect and it is said that they do not require supporting. Cropping starts during September and will continue well into October, possibly November in favourable autumns. Because of the compact growth it is suggested that this raspberry should be allowed to develop into a row of 18–24 ins. width rather than in the orthodox narrow row.

The best alternative to 'September' is probably 'Lloyd George'. Even when grown for summer fruiting the new young canes of this cultivar will frequently produce fruit in the autumn. If not required the flowers can be picked off before the fruit develops, although there is no evidence to show that the autumn fruit detracts from the following summer's crops.

Pests

APHIDS (greenfly). Several species of aphid may be found on raspberries and allied fruits. They cause damage by distorting leaves and young canes. The raspberry aphid and the rubus aphid (Pl. 3, p. 24) are responsible for the spread of certain virus diseases and their satisfactory control is most important.

Control. Either spray in mid-winter with tar oil, or in spring before the flowers open with dimethoate or malathion. The two latter sprays can be used during the summer should this prove necessary, but makers' instructions must be strictly observed where fruit is ripening – the requisite clearance period must be allowed between spraying and picking.

RASPBERRY BEETLE. Routine spraying should keep this pest well under control. Failure to do so may soon lead to a serious build-up and make much of the crop quite uneatable. As such it can be the most serious pest of raspberries and allied fruits. The beetles emerge in May, after hibernating in the soil, and lay their eggs in the flower centres. As the fruits ripen so the newly hatched grubs feed on them (Pl. 21) and burrow inside. The pest is a particularly nasty one, since the grubs frequently are not noticed until the fruit has been prepared for use.

Control. By spraying with derris or malathion just as the first fruits are beginning to colour. Malathion has the added advantage of killing any aphids or leafhoppers that are present, both of which spread virus diseases.

BIRDS. Protection of the ripening fruit is invariably necessary (see p. 11). Fortunately overwintering buds do not seem to be affected.

CANE MIDGE. Young canes are affected. The midge is very small and after emerging from the soil in late spring it proceeds to lay

21. Raspberry beetle larva causing damage to fruit.

eggs in cracks or injuries at the base of the canes. The small grubs that hatch then feed on the cane and cause brownish black blotches. Fungal infections frequently gain entry through the scars and considerable numbers of canes can die during the following winter as a result. Cultivars vary in susceptibility to attack – 'Malling Enterprise' is very susceptible, 'Norfolk Giant' is resistant.

Control. Spray the young canes with gamma-BHC when adult midges first start laying eggs, which is usually about the first week in May. Repeat two weeks later.

CAPSID. Occasionally serious damage to the young canes can be caused by the capsid bug injuring the tips. The injured canes either stop growing or form branches. Slight damage in the form of brown puckered spots and punctures can often be seen on foliage, but control measures should not be necessary unless damage is becoming serious.

Control. If the pest has proved really troublesome spray with DDT in early May. However, as mentioned, this is not generally necessary.

Diseases (other than Virus)

BOTRYTIS. The disease that causes such losses in strawberry crops can also affect raspberries but it is not usually troublesome. It is encouraged by over-close planting, or by keeping too many canes so that not enough air penetrates the foliage in wet seasons. In consequence fruit quickly goes mouldy with approaching ripeness and much of it may be spoilt. Occasionally the disease can kill the canes themselves.

Control. Basically, adequate spacing of the canes is the answer. Should spraying be necessary, use captan, applying it as the first flowers open and again two weeks later. (Where fruit is intended for canning captan should not be used.) Any dead canes should always be cut out and burnt as soon as they are noticed.

CANE BLIGHT. When fruiting canes suddenly wither and die during the summer this disease should be suspected. Infected canes usually snap off easily just above soil level and the incidence of the trouble is sometimes linked with a previous attack of cane midge, damage from which allows the cane blight fungus to enter the canes.

Control. All dead canes should be removed and burnt, cutting away as much of the stump of the cane as possible. This is important where canes have snapped, for it is the stump that will spread the trouble if not removed. Knives or secateurs will carry the infection and should be disinfected. Since cane midge may be a forerunner of cane blight this pest should be controlled where it shows signs of building up (see p. 87). Also, since contaminated soil is a source, no young canes should be used from infected plantations. This is another point in favour of buying certified stock.

CANE SPOT. This disease is quite widespread, particularly in wet summers. Raspberries often perform adequately in spite of it but in some cases they may be seriously weakened Canes, leaves and flower stalks are at first purple-spotted, but later the spots turn greyish white at the centre with purple edges and may be as much as 1 in. across. The more the spotting, the greater the weakening effect, particularly on young developing canes.

Control. Lime sulphur at 5 per cent (2 pints in 5 gallons of water) as the cane buds are bursting and before leaves unfold. Repeat in serious outbreaks at half this strength (1 pint in 5 gallons) just before blossoming. As an alternative use copper fungicide such as Bordeaux mixture (see p. 29). Badly infected canes should be removed and burnt.

SPUR BLIGHT. Like cane spot, this disease is widespread, but usually it is less serious. Buds on the young canes become infected and the cane area adjacent to them turns purplish on the unripened wood then to greyish white in winter. In the following spring infected buds fail to develop. Thus, although canes are seldom killed, fruiting potential may be affected if infection is widespread.

Control. Badly affected canes should be cut out and burnt. This process should start with young canes in summer, following it up when tying-in and again as growth starts the following year. Spraying with Bordeaux mixture or lime sulphur (as for cane spot) should be tried where spur blight is really troublesome. There is also evidence that the use of captan as advised for botrytis (p. 29) gives a good control.

22. Raspberry shoots showing symptoms of a virus disease.

Virus Diseases

The seriousness of these diseases is emphasized again, and the reader is referred in particular to Chapter 3. Not all the virus diseases affecting raspberries are spread by aphids (greenfly). Leafhoppers are responsible in at least one instance, and in others small eelworms in the soil render certain virus diseases 'soil-borne' in some districts.

The recognition of the different viruses affecting raspberries is not easy and certainly not within the scope of this book. The same virus may cause varying reaction and symptoms in different cultivars. Probably the most widespread virus disease is the one known as mosaic, which usually produces some form of irregular yellow mottling or spotting of the leaves (Pl. 22). The leaves do not develop properly as a result and may become distorted and crumpled, and cane growth becomes stunted and unprofitable, sometimes within one or two seasons, sometimes over a protracted period.

Raspberry yellow dwarf virus is another possible disease and causes a line pattern on foliage plus stunting of the canes. Some raspberries, e.g. 'Malling Jewel', are virtually immune to this virus.

Yet again, a virus disease known as stunt and dwarf can cause severe stunting of canes. As this trouble is spread by leafhoppers the control of these by malathion is advised.

8 · Blackberries, Loganberries and Other Hybrid Berries

This chapter will deal basically with cultivated blackberries and loganberries, but other desirable hybrid berries are listed on p. 98. Whatever fruits are chosen, the conditions required for success are much the same.

Site

Almost any site will do providing the soil is reasonably good, although more favourable positions will obviously produce better and heavier crops. Blackberries and hybrid berries are particularly suited to shaded and north-facing walls, boundary fences and archways which may be unsuitable for other fruits. Although several thornless forms are available, the majority of cultivars possess wicked thorns and it is well to position the plants away from frequently used pathways.

Spring frosts are no problem, since these fruits are the last to flower, but winter hardiness is another matter. Loganberries, particularly the thornless form and the boysenberry, can be badly killed back in severe winters, although the stock usually survives below ground and more often than not recovers.

Soil

Whilst the more vigorous cultivars will hold their own on all but the very worst soils, the weaker ones will not. In general the thornless forms seem to lack strength and usually show signs of stress where the soil is not good enough. Thus the 'Himalaya' blackberry and ordinary loganberry may put up a brave show on poor thin ground, but the 'Merton Thornless' blackberry and 'Thornless Loganberry' will not thrive unaided for long in similar circumstances.

Preparation

Generally speaking, soils have much the same effect on black-berries and hybrid berries as on raspberries, and as these plants will occupy the ground for ten or fifteen years, or sometimes longer, it is important to prepare adequately. On lighter and certainly on alkaline soils it is essential to dig in plenty of well-rotted manure and compost. Prepare the ground thoroughly and deeply and the plants will respond by remaining a worthwhile proposition for a proportionately longer period. Basically, follow the preparation details outlined for raspberries on p. 74.

Support

Some form of support is essential. Without it plants become a tangled mass of canes which is difficult if not impossible to un-ravel. Galvanized piping is probably the best material to use for uprights, as it lasts so much longer than wood. If wood is used, seasoned sweet chestnut is one of the best for lasting wear, especially if the base is soaked in a solution of copper sulphate (2 lb. in 10 gallons of water) for 48 hours. Support wires can be attached to the uprights at 1-ft intervals up to a height of about $5\frac{1}{2}$ ft, the lowest at about $2\frac{1}{2}$ ft from the ground. Ideally the wire ends should be attached to straining eyes so that any slack can be taken up as necessary. Where plants are to be trained against walls or fences the wires will need to be threaded through vine eyes driven into the brick or wood work. Staples are not so satisfactory as they often pull out too easily.

Source

With virus troubles a distinct possibility a reliable source for plants is important. There is a certification scheme in operation for the latest selection of loganberry and a recent selection of thornless loganberry may possibly be included too. While there is no certification scheme for other hybrid berries or blackberries, reputable growers make it their business to propagate only the best and healthiest stock, and in purchasing from such firms one is taking a sensible safeguard.

It must be emphasized that just because a plant is healthy when taken from the nursery it will not necessarily remain im-mune to virus troubles afterwards. Thus any unhealthy black-berry, raspberry, loganberry or allied plants should be burnt *before* the new plants come in. Also, since certain viruses are soil-borne (via eelworms), it is always advisable to choose a fresh planting site for replacements.

Planting

This can be done any time between October and early March when weather and soil conditions are suitable, the earlier the better. The young plants should be placed carefully in the planting hole with roots well spread (see Pl. 57, p. 164) and the soil gradually packed firmly around them. The nursery soil-mark on the short piece of cane above the roots will indicate depth of planting, the buds above the roots usually resting 1–2 ins. below the surface.

Where more than one plant is required, a minimum of 6 ft should be allowed between plants for weak growers like 'Merton Thornless' and 'Denver Thornless' blackberries, but 10 or even 12 ft for 'Himalaya' blackberry and loganberry. If more than one row is needed allow 7 ft between rows.

Training and Tying-in

After planting cut down any existing cane to 9 ins. above ground. Usually only one or two canes are produced in the first summer, but autumn plantings invariably develop rather more than later ones. These young canes must be preserved uninjured and should be trained up to and then along the top wire with fillis string as they develop.

23. Various methods of training loganberries, etc. Solid lines represent fruiting canes, which will be cut out after cropping. Dotted lines are young canes. In the top and bottom examples young canes are lowered to take the place of older canes after pruning. In the other examples the positions of young and old alternate.

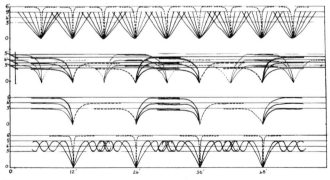

It is at this stage that some form of training should be adopted whereby only half the wire space is used up (Pl. 23). The reason for this is that both from the health and pruning point of view it is best to keep old and young canes separate. The idea finding most favour is to train the young canes more or less upright with the fruiting canes forming a fan on either side of them. Once the latter have finished fruiting they are cut away and the young canes are lowered and trained fan-wise in their place. The centre is then left vacant to receive further young canes a year later. In this way the young canes are always held *above* the older fruiting canes and are not so easily infected by any disease that may be present on the older parts of the plant. The foregoing is only one of a number of possible training methods (see Pl. 23).

Tying-in of the young canes, where their position needs to be changed after pruning, is best delayed until late February to early March, so that any that may have been damaged or killed by winter cold can be cut out.

Picking

Fruit should be ripe but not soft ripe if it is to be preserved, and should be gathered when quite dry. As with raspberries, mould will form very quickly in humid weather and any wetness among the fruits will cause rapid deterioration – often within hours of picking.

There is one major difference between the gathering of raspberries and that of blackberries and loganberries. With raspberries (see p. 81) the fruit 'pulls off' the core, which is left behind still attached to the stalk on the cane; with blackberries and loganberries the white core comes away with the fruit and forms part of the edible whole. But it should be emphasized that for exhibition purposes all *Rubus* fruits (raspberries, loganberries boysenberries, etc.) must be cut *complete with stalk and calyx*, about an inch from the fruit.

Pruning

The pruning of newly planted specimens and general directions for training are described on page 94. Thereafter regular pruning is important, for without it growth soon becomes a tangled, impenetrable mass. The operation is quite simple technically, for all that is entailed is the removal of the old canes after they have finished fruiting (Pl. 24). Certain blackberries will fruit

24. Old and new canes of blackberry. The old are pruned out after fruiting and the new take their place. The same treatment applies to loganberries, etc.

over and over again on the same cane, but the retention of old canes is not recommended, since the overall vigour of the plant may suffer and new growths become less numerous in consequence. From the practical angle, of course, gloves are necessary, and the job is made much easier if two people do it – one holding and pulling away the prunings as the second person cuts. The very long canes are best cut into several portions to facilitate their removal to the fire heap.

Untrained specimens can present a real pruning problem and it is largely for this reason that blackberries and loganberries should be grown on specially provided supports and wires, training one or more canes to each wire.

As far as possible new canes should arise from ground level or thereabouts. Only if such material is insufficient for requirements should young canes emanating from older wood be retained.

Frequently there is a certain amount of dieback at the tips of the young canes by the end of the winter. These tips should be removed in late February to early March to a point where a live bud exists and where the wood is perfectly clean and unmarked. Any dead or obviously unhealthy canes should be removed in the same operation.

Manuring

Since the production of adequate young cane is vital, soil conditions must be conducive to this. Normally, annual dressings of rotted farmyard manure in spring should be all that is required; the lighter or more alkaline the soil the more important does this become. General directions for the use of manures and fertilizers are as for raspberries (p. 83) and the comments on and recommendations for any deficiency troubles equally apply.

Watering

This can make all the difference in some areas between an excellent crop and a mediocre one. If the soil lacks adequate moisture it must be remembered that *two* crops are threatened – the currently developing one and the potential one for the following year in the form of the new canes. Again, much the same applies as for raspberries (p. 84).

Cultivars

A. *Blackberries*

The following blackberries, all of which are self-fertile, are listed in one or other of current fruit nurserymen's catalogues.

BEDFORD GIANT. Ripens late July–August, juicy and sweet, growth vigorous.

MERTON EARLY. Ripens early – mid-August, good flavour, growth moderate, heavy cropper.

HIMALAYA. Ripens mid-August onwards, fair flavour and often rather acid, growth extremely vigorous and requires regular attention to keep under control on better soils; heavy cropper.

PARSLEY-LEAVED or CUT-LEAF BLACKBERRY (*Rubus laciniatus*). Ripens late August onwards, one of the best-flavoured cultivated blackberries, vigorous only under good soil conditions. As the name indicates the foliage is distinctive and is quite decorative.

OREGON THORNLESS. This is a thornless form of the parsley-leaved blackberry and was introduced from the U.S.A. Like its relative, good soil conditions are essential for best results. Period of ripening and other details as for parsley-leaved.

MERTON THORNLESS. Ripens August, fair flavour, growth often too weak except under good conditions.

JOHN INNES. Ripens late August and continues fruiting for several weeks, good flavour, growth fairly vigorous, heavy cropper.

B. *Hybrid Berries*

The following are the best known, but only those marked * appear in current lists to hand.

*BOYSENBERRY. Origin, California about 1930. Supposedly a loganberry–blackberry–raspberry hybrid. Fruits large and deep red, prized for cooking. The boysenberry is subject to winter killing in severe conditions.

*JAPANESE WINEBERRY (*Rubus phoenicolasius*). Highly decorative orange-red fruits surrounded by an equally colourful calyx and borne on canes covered with wine-coloured spines. Edible, but of little merit in this sense. Growth similar to raspberry.

KING'S ACRE BERRY. Resembles a blackberry; fruit large and long, ripens during early July. Now seldom if ever seen. Liable to winter killing.

*LOGANBERRY. Origin, U.S.A. Said to be a cross between a raspberry (American type) and a blackberry, with dark red berries larger than those of either parent. Ripens mid-July to August. Growth vigorous, heavy cropper. Probably the most widely cultivated *Rubus* fruit in Great Britain after the raspberry. Although acid for fresh dessert, the flavour when cooked or preserved is superb. Worthy of a trial in any garden, the only disadvantage being the thorns. (There is a thornless form – see below.) The clone raised jointly by East Malling and Long Ashton Research Stations in 1959 and known as LY 59 is the best available.

LOWBERRY. Origin California. A blackberry–dewberry hybrid. Like a loganberry, but has sweeter fruits, which are nearly black and approaching 2 ins. in length. Liable to damage from winter frosts and seldom listed.

MALLING HYBRID. 53–16. Raised at East Malling Research Station. Prized by those who know it for jam-making. The seeds are less troublesome than of most raspberries or hybrid berries. Purplish black fruits are borne on canes similar to blackberry.

*NECTARBERRY. Fruit dark crimson and said to be of good flavour. Growth moderate.

PHENOMENAL BERRY. Resembles the loganberry with slightly larger fruits. Seldom listed.

STRAWBERRY–RASPBERRY (*Rubus illecebrosus*). Produces short, erect canes 6–15 ins. long which bear colourful red fruits in late summer. These are very insipid eaten fresh but are said to make delicious jam.

*THORNLESS LOGANBERRY (BAUER'S). Developed in California. Season as for loganberry. Very similar to the ordinary loganberry apart from the absence of thorns. The foliage is a slightly lighter green in colour and growth is rather less vigorous. An excellent subject for garden cultivation. Widely listed.

N.B.: There seems every likelihood that before long an East Malling selection of the 'Thornless Loganberry' (possibly a derivative of Bauer's form) will become available, and may well prove to be the loganberry of the future.

*VEITCHBERRY. Origin, England. A blackberry–raspberry cross. Fruit is very large, finely flavoured and the colour of a ripe mulberry. Ripens during July.

*WORCESTER BERRY. Related to the gooseberry; see page 132.

YOUNGBERRY. Origin, California. Supposedly a blackberry–dewberry cross. Very large reddish black fruits, juicy and of fine flavour. The canes can be killed in severe winters.

Pests

Any pests usually found are in common with those that may affect raspberries.

APHIDS. The chief danger here lies in the spread of virus disease by these pests. Control measures as for raspberries (see p. 87). The winter tar oil should be applied as an annual routine treatment.

BIRDS. Fortunately, birds are not usually so attracted to blackberries and hybrid berries as to raspberries. Should any trouble be experienced netting over is of course the answer.

RASPBERRY BEETLE (Pl. 21, p. 88). This is probably the most serious pest for blackberries and loganberries as well as for raspberries. For general details see p. 87.

Control. The same substances may be used as on raspberries, but timing is different since flowering of blackberries etc. is somewhat later than that of raspberries. *Blackberries.* One spray is usually sufficient applying it as the first flowers open. *Loganberries.* Two sprays may be necessary here, the first approximately mid-June, when flowering is nearly over, the second two weeks later, as first fruits begin to colour.

Diseases

Cane spot and spur blight occur on loganberries and other hybrids, the former occasionally on blackberries. Control measures as recommended for raspberries (p. 90).

Virus Diseases

STUNT (*Dwarf*). A serious virus among blackberries, loganberries and other hybrid berries as well as raspberries. Many thin, dwarfed growths are produced and infected plants may die. The virus is spread by a leafhopper, the control of which is aided by the use of malathion against raspberry beetle in June to early July.

Other viruses may affect blackberries, loganberries and hybrid berries besides stunt, and routine measures against aphids and a change of site in any replanting are recommended for maintaining healthy plants.

9 · Blackcurrants

Anyone with a garden who complains of the high price of black-currants in the shops surely deserves to pay for them! Here is a fruit native to Europe and well suited to our climate that is neglected to a puzzling degree. Indeed, a good garden sample of blackcurrants is a rarity and the inevitable conclusion is that, dis-couraged by poor results many gardeners give up in despair. It is safe to say that most of them would be pleasantly surprised at the improved results if only one or two basic points of cultivation were regularly satisfied.

The value of blackcurrants for their vitamin C content and the uses to which this fruit can be put render it one of the most valuable and important fruits one can grow. Jam, jelly, juice, bottled and deep-frozen samples are all exceptionally nourishing and appetizing for the long winter months, and a few well-grown bushes should produce more than sufficient fruit for the average household's requirements.

Site

The chief requirement is shelter from cold winds. The black-currant flowers early, in March or April, depending on the season, and unless the flowers are adequately pollinated much of the crop may be lost. The cold winds so often prevailing at this period restrict visits from bees and other pollinating insects. Naturally therefore the warmer and quieter the site the more likely is there to be good insect activity and therefore good pollination. This is particularly important for cultivars which rely more on the mechanical transfer of pollen by insects because of the position-ing of their flower parts. This point is discussed more fully under 'Fertility' on p. 111.

Like most of our hardy fruits blackcurrants are very liable to damage from spring frosts. As just mentioned, March to April flowering has to be reckoned with and this means that for nearly two months there is a risk of frost. It should not be difficult however to give some protection in one way or another and suggestions to this end are made on p. 15. For preference an open sunny situation should be chosen, but blackcurrants are not averse to some shade if it cannot be avoided.

Soil

Obviously the weight of crop is related to soil type and fertility, and one will – or should – always get higher returns from the better moisture-holding soils. But with adequate preparation and aftercare thoroughly worthwhile quantities of good fruit can be picked from bushes on less favourable soils too, for ten, even fifteen years and more.

The foregoing comments apply particularly to light sands and gravels as well as to chalky soils, where adequate humus is vital if normal growth and performance are to be maintained.

Plenty of moisture during the summer is essential and regular attention to manuring will do much to take care of this. Watering has long since been shown to be of immense value to black-currants and this too is vital. Having emphasized the need for moisture it must be realized that on heavier, poorly drained soils trouble is likely to occur sooner or later. While blackcurrants may not be as sensitive as some crops are to these adverse conditions they will never thrive under them.

Preparation for Planting

In an established garden this should present no problem. The digging-in of generous quantities of well-rotted manure and/or compost is still necessary though, bearing in mind that it will not be possible once planting has been done, for anyone who digs through a bed of blackcurrants is doing far more harm than good. On well-worked soil single-digging should be adequate but unbroken ground will require more extensive preparation in the form of double-digging, which will break up the soil to a good depth to allow a full root run.

There is no adequate substitute here for rotted farmyard manure or compost, but if supplies are out of the question then the digging-in of peat plus bone meal and hoof and horn meal each at 3 oz. per sq. yd and sulphate of potash at 1 oz. are recommended, scuffling them into the top few inches of soil.

Weedy ground, as always, should be treated with suspicion. Annuals like groundsel and chickweed can easily be skimmed off and dug in with the manure. Pernicious perennials on the other hand should be completely eradicated before attempting to plant.

The ground should preferably be prepared well in advance of planting, and as planting is done from late October to early November onwards it should normally be fairly easy to have things ready in good time. The great danger of late preparation, particularly with double-digging, is that the ground will be insufficiently firm to allow quick establishment of the root system.

Blackcurrants are averse to excessively acid soil conditions and a pH of around 6·0 should be the aim. Occasional soil tests to determine the pH reading are well worthwhile, particularly if crops are not satisfactory, and a reading of less than 5·7 should be the signal for a light application of lime. A safe dressing would be 3–4 oz. per sq. yd of ground chalk or 2–3 oz. of hydrated lime scattered evenly over the surface. An alternative would be the use of fertilizers containing free lime such as Nitro Chalk and Nitra Shell (see p. 42).

Buying Bushes

It is very important to buy healthy bushes. Unlike virus diseases in strawberries and raspberries, which usually have a stunting effect on the plants, the reversion virus (see p. 116) on blackcurrants is not so obvious. Growth is reasonable but crops become poor, soon non-existent, and this may well be the prime reason for the inexplicable absence of blackcurrants from so many gardens.

The importance of purchasing *certified* bushes from a source advertising them as such cannot be over-emphasized. This is as sure a way as any of gaining success. To accept cuttings from bushes of uncertain health status or to retain old unhealthy bushes will almost certainly lead to disappointment. The reversion virus is spread by a minute but very troublesome pest called the blackcurrant gall mite, or more commonly, big bud mite, and it is nearly always present in poorly grown bushes. The best way to protect young bushes from big bud is to spray with lime sulphur, as outlined on p. 29.

Planting

Two-year-old bushes are usually the best specimens for planting and these are what the nurserymen would normally supply. Good one-year-old specimens are however quite acceptable (Pl. 25).

Any time between late October and early February is suitable,

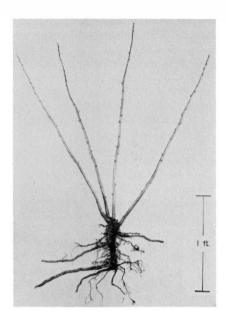

25. A good two-year-old blackcurrant bush suitable for planting.

I ft.

the earlier the better. Bushes can be planted later, but growth in the first season will usually suffer as a result. Blackcurrant bushes are one of the few fruits which benefit from low planting, that is placing the bush at a slightly deeper level than that at which it had previously been growing. This is because the bush is grown as a 'stool', with a succession of young shoots produced annually from or even below ground level. Thus, low planting ensures a maximum number of buds below the soil from which successive supplies of young shoots will come. It is dangerous however to plant too deeply and the bushes should only be set 1 in. to 2 ins. deeper than the original nursery soil-mark. Equally it is a mistake to plant them high, which will only expose basal buds and prevent the correct formation of the bush on the stool method.

As always, soil and weather conditions must be right, and it is much better to delay planting than to risk working on wet or partially frozen ground.

Planting distances usually quoted for gardens are 5 ft between bushes and 6 ft between rows. Where space is limited the commercial growers' layout of a hedgerow plant certainly allows for

26. A newly planted blackcurrant, pruned.

easier picking and general maintenance if a quantity of black-currants are to be grown. This is particularly the case in wet summers, where 5 ft × 6 ft planting may lead to overcrowding and mouldy fruit. With the hedgerow system bushes are rather closer in the row, but with 2–3 ft more between rows. Thus, a plant of 4 ft in rows × 8 ft between or 3½ ft × 9 ft might be considered.

Pruning after Planting

It may appear drastic, but the correct treatment is to cut *all* growth down to, at the most, two buds above soil level (Pl. 26). It is wrong to leave the shoots any longer than this, worse still to leave them unpruned. By pruning severely one is ensuring that the bush has a full season in which to establish itself before being called upon to crop. Newly planted bushes can be pruned imme-diately or, failing this, by the end of February.

Pruning One Year after Planting

Providing soil and other conditions have been satisfactory a blackcurrant bush may well produce six good shoots during the first summer, maybe more. These are the shoots that will fruit the following year and they should *not* be pruned in any way. In fact this is one occasion in the life of a blackcurrant bush when little or no pruning should be necessary. All that may be needed is the cutting back to a bud near ground level of any thin wispy shoots or any that happen to be growing out at awkward horizontal angles.

Pruning Established Bushes

It is at this point that many people shy away from pruning, not knowing where to begin. Consequently bushes gradually become more and more congested and the amount of new growth becomes less and less in proportion to the old (Pl. 27). And with the falling-off in new growth comes a falling-off in cropping, both in quantity and size of fruit.

Admittedly a fully established blackcurrant bush can look rather puzzling to anyone not familiar with pruning. Yet, as in most cases, an understanding of the way in which the bush fruits will quickly lead to an understanding of the way in which it should be pruned. Most of the fruit on a blackcurrant bush is produced on the shoots that grew in the previous year or, as it is commonly called, one-year-old wood. A little fruit comes on older wood but the bulk of it, and certainly the best, is on the one-year-old shoots (Pl. 27). Meanwhile new shoots will be growing, many of them from at or near ground level. These are the shoots that will give next year's fruit.

Thus, immediately after picking the ripe fruit the bush will largely consist of (a) shoots that have just fruited and (b) young, newly formed shoots. Pruning should quite simply involve the removal of as much of category (a) shoots as possible, retaining the best of category (b). What can so often confuse is the fact that young shoots arise from various points on the one-year-old fruiting shoots as well as from nearer ground level. The answer of course is that inevitably some of the new shoots have to be sacrificed in the removal of wood that has fruited.

Bearing the above points in mind, it is well to remember that as much of the new wood as possible should originate from or within twelve inches or so of ground level (Pls. 28, 29). And where basal portions of older wood are retained because they are carrying useful young shoots, they should not be kept for more than

27. (*Left*) Good blackcurrant shoots from the summer's growth called 'one year old'. These should be retained for the following year's crop. (*Centre and right*) Older shoots that have fruited. These must be cut out from as low a point as possible (Pls. 28, 29). Some young wood at the shoot tips must inevitably be sacrificed in the process.

28. A young blackcurrant bush, unpruned.
29. The same bush pruned. A large bush would carry four or five times the number of shoots.

2–3 years before being cut right out, either using a pruning saw or pruning shears (Pl. 62, p. 173). Any such large cuts may benefit from a coating of bituminous tree paint to prevent rotting.

The time of pruning is often dictated by what time one has to spare. Ideally blackcurrant bushes should be pruned immediately after the fruit has been picked. Remaining growths are then given a full ration of sun and air for their development. Even so, excellent results are still obtained where pruning is delayed until the winter. There is, therefore, more than half a year in which pruning can be done, and one advantage in winter pruning is that the old and young wood can be more easily distinguished. A useful guide is that the young shoots to be retained are always the lightest in colour.

A system or method of pruning is advisable and the following is recommended:

(a) Remove all low-hanging growth, both young and old. If left to fruit the crop will only drag on the soil and rot.

(b) Remove older wood from the remainder of the bush.

(c) Cut out all small shoots from the centre of the bush.

Protecting the Fruit

This is not always essential, but where blackbirds, thrushes or pigeons are numerous much of the crop can soon disappear. Damage can start quite early with the first sign of colour on the fruit, and one should be prepared to net the bushes from early July on. Some posts with support strings or wires are advisable, otherwise young growth may be injured by the net.

Picking

Generally speaking blackcurrants should be picked when an overall black in colour. However, several first early sorts (e.g. 'Boskoop Giant' and 'Mendip X') may start dropping some of the fruit if they are left until terminal berries blacken. In such cases it is preferable to pick the fruit firm ripe, even if one or two of the small terminal fruits are still pinkish purple. On the other hand the late cultivars, such as 'Baldwin' and 'Amos Black', will hang on the bush (given suitable protection) for several weeks providing conditions are not too wet.

Fruit should be picked dry, particularly if it is not for immediate use. It should also be picked complete with strig, not as individual berries. Some of the mid-season and late-ripening cultivars may ripen unevenly and require picking in two stages.

Manuring

Without good quantities of new growth each season bushes cannot possibly crop to capacity, for, as has been seen, it is on this new growth that the bulk of the following season's crop will come. It is therefore vital to feed blackcurrants regularly, and the best way of doing this is with an annual spring mulch of rotted farmyard manure, compost or straw. Some fertilizers are also very helpful: sulphate of ammonia at 1 to $1\frac{1}{2}$ oz. per sq. yd (using Nitro Chalk in lieu on acid soil) plus sulphate of potash at $\frac{1}{2}$ to 1 oz. per sq. yd are advised each February, and an occasional dressing of bone meal or superphosphate at 3 oz. per sq. yd, say every other year, helps to maintain reserves of phosphates.

Watering

Adequate moisture is vital for good results, otherwise full use cannot be made of any manures or fertilizers given. This applies to a greater or lesser degree to most fruits but *in particular* to those like the blackcurrant where the following year's crop is dependent on plenty of young growth. Watering must be done early enough to assist both the developing crop and the new growth. Apply the equivalent of at least 1 in. of rainfall, which is $4\frac{1}{2}$ gallons per sq. yd (for the calculation of this see p. 23).

Weeding

Blackcurrants in good fettle should succeed in smothering most weeds. A spring mulch also helps to do this. Deep-rooted kinds like bindweed and bryony, however, can be very troublesome and need quick action to be kept regularly under control (see p. 170).

Roguing

Each season careful watch should be kept for any abnormalities. Are some bushes cropping less than others and are they different in appearance? If so, reversion virus should be suspected and expert advice sought. Full details are given on p. 116.

Cultivars

There is a fine range of cultivars from which to choose. Where several bushes are to be planted it is a distinct advantage to select cultivars that ripen in succession, unless the fruit is specifically required at one time. As an example, 'Boskoop Giant' is one of the first to ripen, 'Wellington XXX' would be about ten days later, 'Baldwin' twenty days and 'Amos Black' as much as thirty days later in ripening.

A. *Blackcurrants Particularly Recommended* (*in approximate order of ripening*).

BOSKOOP GIANT. Earliest to ripen. Large fruits which drop quickly once black. Pick when terminal berries are still pink. A good cultivar for exhibition but cropping is markedly reduced by adverse spring weather.

LAXTON'S GIANT. Early. One of the largest-fruited blackcurrants.

TOR CROSS. Early. A new blackcurrant raised at Long Ashton Research Station, Bristol. Very promising and worthy of trial.

WELLINGTON XXX. Early mid-season. Raised at East Malling Research Station, Kent, in 1913, this is one of the most widely successful blackcurrants grown. Fruit should be picked as soon as fully coloured, otherwise some may be lost as it quickly drops.

SEABROOK'S BLACK. Mid-season. Very good where it succeeds but like 'Boskoop Giant' may be disappointing unless weather is favourable during and after flowering.

RAVEN. Mid-season. This comparatively old blackcurrant has recently come to the fore following good results in trials.

BLACKSMITH (LAXTON'S). Mid-season. A blackcurrant that has done consistently well in various trials. Deserves to be more widely grown. Long truss of fruit and good exhibition currant.

BALDWIN. Late. Widely grown commercially, primarily for the production of concentrated juice. High in vitamin C and a very good currant but not the heaviest of croppers. Makes a smaller bush than most and can be planted a little closer than other cultivars. The particular selection known as 'Hilltop Baldwin' is generally held to be the best. Varies in performance.

WESTWICK CHOICE. Late. A very useful alternative to 'Baldwin' though fruit tends to turn mouldy very quickly in wet weather.

DANIEL'S SEPTEMBER BLACK. Very late. Very similar to 'Baldwin', from which it probably originated as a variant or sport. Indeed, bushes (or parts of them) of Daniel's sometimes revert to being 'Baldwin' and the cultivar is now less popular because

110

of this unreliability. True, Daniel's ripens a week or so later than 'Baldwin' and the fruit will remain firm without dropping over a considerable period.

AMOS BLACK. Very late. Generally not a heavy cropper but a useful alternative to 'Daniel's September Black' for extending the season. Flowers late and should be a choice for frosty gardens.

B. *Other blackcurrants less widely grown but occasionally listed.*

DAVISON'S EIGHT. Mid-season.

GOLIATH. Mid-season. Closely resembles 'Victoria', from which it was selected.

LAXTON'S NIGGER. Mid-season.

VICTORIA. Mid-season.

LAXTON'S GRAPE. Mid-season to late.

MALVERN CROSS. Late.

Cultivars with highest vitamin C include 'Baldwin', 'Blacksmith', 'Boskoop Giant', 'Daniel's September Black', 'Laxton's Giant' and 'Raven'.

Fertility

Blackcurrant cultivars vary in their ability to set and develop a crop. Some, such as 'Boskoop Giant' and 'Seabrook's Black', have a marked susceptibility to cold conditions (possibly through lack of leafy cover for the flowers); some apparently suffer from a positioning of the flower parts that does not favour self-pollination. Therefore unless conditions are suitable for pollinating insects to operate a poor set of fruit may result.

It is an advantage to grow a mixture of cultivars together. This leads to considerable cross-pollination and heavier crops can result in consequence. The growing of several cultivars to give a longer picking season has already been mentioned, and this idea would automatically reap the benefit of improved cross-pollination.

Pests

The control of certain blackcurrant pests is important on two counts. Firstly, any check to new growth will inevitably reduce cropping and, secondly, failure to control blackcurrant gall mite will result sooner or later in bushes becoming infected with reversion virus disease.

APHIDS (greenfly). These are a common sight on bushes in late spring or early summer. Their effect in bad infestations can be serious, since the young shoots are distorted and leaves curled. A bush so affected would bear a reduced crop not only that year but inevitably also a year later because of the irreparable damage to the young shoots.

Control. A tar-oil winter wash in December or early January annually. If an infestation begins to develop in spring in spite of tar oil then use malathion or dimethoate (though not using the latter within a week of picking).

BIG BUD. See blackcurrant gall mite, below.

BIRDS. Damage to the fruit is more than likely. Damage to the opening buds is more localized but can be devastating when it occurs. Bullfinches and sparrows are the chief offenders, and bushes should be protected with fruit nets as required.

BLACKCURRANT GALL MITE. Without question the most serious pest of blackcurrants because of its association with reversion virus, which it spreads. It is also the most common. The mites are microscopic in size and many thousands may be found in a single infested bud. Such buds are rounded and swollen beyond normal size and are easily seen during the winter (Pl. 30). A really effective means of control has still not been found but the following measures are advised.

Control. Spray twice each spring with lime sulphur at 1 per cent strength ($\frac{1}{4}$ pt in 3 gallons of water) plus a spreader. The first application should be given as the first flowers open, and the treatment repeated three weeks later. All cultivars should tolerate this treatment (scorch can occur on some if higher concentrations of lime sulphur are used). The spraying *must* be done regularly and thoroughly from the very first season so that the pest is prevented from gaining a foothold. Badly infested bushes are a bad risk and should be dug up and burnt.

BLACKCURRANT LEAF MIDGE (LEAF-CURLING MIDGE). Not of great importance in gardens, although the typical crimping to-

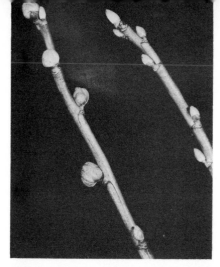

30. Blackcurrant gall mite. (*Left*) Infested buds. (*Right*) Normal buds.

gether of one or two leaves at the tips of young shoots can reduce growth slightly in bad attacks. The damage appears during June and July, the injured leaf turning a brownish colour.

Control. A drenching spray of DDT as first flowers open, repeated three weeks later. This treatment should only be necessary where a serious build-up is likely.

BLACKCURRANT SAWFLY. Occasionally voracious green and black caterpillars (similar to those in Pl. 49, p. 146) denude much of the foliage almost overnight. Steps should be taken at the first sign of trouble, damage usually occurring during June and more often than not in the centre or on the underside of the bush.

Control. Spray with derris at the first sign of damage.

CAPSIDS. Not usually a very serious threat to garden blackcurrants except locally. The overwintering eggs on the shoots hatch in spring and the green bugs suck the sap from the growing shoot tips. Tiny brownish-yellow holes result and develop into larger scars, causing puckered areas as the leaves grow (Pl. 31).

Control. A spray of DDT at grape-bud stage (Pl. 32). This should be necessary only where bad attacks have occurred.

CLEARWING MOTH. Seldom causes sufficient damage to be of any consequence and in any case there is no easy means of controlling it. The larvae feed by tunnelling down the centre of

113

31. Damage on blackcurrant foliage caused by capsids. Red and white currants and gooseberries are similarly affected.

32. The grape-bud stage of flower truss in black-currants – just before the first flowers open.

shoots and occasionally a shoot tip may be seen to wilt. The hollow shoots are more noticeable at pruning time and if any are seen this note may serve as an explanation for their presence.

RED SPIDER MITE. Serious infestations of the glasshouse red spider can sometimes occur in seasons that happen to be favourable to it. Leaves are quickly bronzed through the loss of sap (the minute red mites feed on the undersides of the leaves) and the bush can be weakened considerably as a result.

Control. Spray with dimethoate in May.

Diseases

Undoubtedly the most serious disease is that of reversion. This is discussed under Virus Diseases, p. 116. One or two diseases as distinct from viruses can be troublesome to a greater or lesser degree:

AMERICAN GOOSEBERRY MILDEW. This disease, familiar to all who have grown gooseberries (p. 148), can and will also attack currants, black, red and white. Indeed, it has become much more serious in commercial plantations and nurseries recently, and it may well affect garden currants more widely too. On blackcurrants the disease affects the tips of young growths during June and July, curling the leaves upward to reveal white powdery areas. In severe cases the fruit also may be covered with mildew.

Control. Regular use of lime sulphur against gall mite (p. 31) should keep mildew at bay. Dinocap can also be used, although lime sulphur is probably more effective. Sprays of washing soda at $\frac{1}{2}$ lb. in $2\frac{1}{2}$ gallons of water plus some soft soap or a proprietary spreader from soon after flowering can also be tried.

BOTRYTIS. The grey mould fungus, as it is commonly called, can seriously affect blackcurrant crops in wet seasons, particularly in crowded plantations. There is also the possibility of the disease causing dieback of branches. (See dieback, below.)

Control. If the fruit is picked as soon as coloured, losses will be greatly reduced. Overcrowding is the real cause of the trouble and pruning should be rather harder where necessary, bearing in mind that wider spacing should be allowed for in any future plantings.

DIEBACK. Occasionally an odd branch or two may die, the rest of the bush remaining quite healthy. A number of organisms can cause this, including botrytis (grey mould) and coral spot.

Control. Cut back to clean healthy wood if possible and burn the affected pieces as soon as they are noticed. Avoid leaving long budless snags at the base of the bush when pruning.

LEAF SPOT. This disease is a particular menace in the higher rainfall areas but can occur in most districts in wetter seasons. Infection is carried over on the fallen leaves, from which masses of spores are released the following spring. Leaves become spotted brown to a greater or lesser degree (compare Pl. 51) depending on the year, and in severe attacks the spots, though only minute, become so numerous that they join up to form larger areas of dead tissue. Diseased leaves are infectious long before they fall and the trouble quickly spreads. The implications of premature leaf fall (certainly by late July, often earlier) are all too clear and bushes are seriously weakened.

Control. Spray with zineb, incorporating it with the lime sulphur spray against gall mite. Repeat the zineb spray once or twice at fortnightly intervals and again after picking where the disease is really troublesome; sprays of Bordeaux mixture can also be used but only *after picking*. Some areas will not require a spray; some cultivars are more prone to the disease than others, but all are susceptible to it. The raking-up and burning of fallen blackcurrant leaves will also help.

RUST. Fairly late in the season the underside of leaves may become covered with masses of raised cinnamon-coloured pustules. This is blackcurrant rust, part of the organism's life taking place on blackcurrants and part on five-needled pines (e.g. *Pinus strobus* and *P. monticola*).

Control. Rust, when it occurs, develops too late in the season to cause any serious trouble. If it developed earlier, like leaf spot, it would be a different matter. Should a spray be necessary use Bordeaux mixture and apply in May and again after fruiting.

Virus Disease

REVERSION. This incurable virus disease is widespread. It goes hand in hand with blackcurrant gall mite ('big bud' mite; see

116

33. Reversion virus disease. (*Left*) Normal leaf. (*Right*) Reverted leaf.

p. 112) and where gall mite is present reversion will soon show. The difficulty lies in the fact that infected bushes at first do not look obviously different from their healthy counterparts, so that in the majority of cases the bushes are retained in the belief that frost or some other adverse condition has severely reduced the crop. In fact such bushes will never again crop satisfactorily and as time goes on the bush does look different, as indeed it is. Compare a leaf from a badly reverted bush with that from a healthy one and the difference becomes obvious.

Means of singling out infected bushes are perhaps not easy to grasp, but if they can be it will mean that infected, unproductive bushes will be cleared out and burnt much sooner than otherwise. Useful ways of identifying reversion include:

(a) Flower bud colour: The unopened flower buds, at the stage of development called grape-bud stage (Pl. 32), should be a *pale* greyish-purple colour. On a bush suffering from reversion the bud is of a *darker* purple and the greyish downy look is absent.

(b) Leaf veins: A blackcurrant leaf consists of three lobes or sections. Healthy leaves should have at least five lateral veins radiating from the mid-rib to the leaf edge on the large central lobe (Pl. 33). If less than five are apparent then the bush is reverted. The symptoms are not apparent until late May or June.

(c) Leaf margin teeth: these may vary in number according to the variety, but a minimum of 13 should be present on one side of the central lobe. If there are less than 13 then reversion is present.

N.B.: The identification of reversion in the early stages, particularly of symptoms (b) and (c), may not be easy, and for garden purposes one should immediately be suspicious when crops fall off in successive seasons for no apparent reason. In such cases expert advice should be sought.

Control. There is none. Infected bushes must be despatched to the bonfire without delay, together with any recently grown progeny from them. The trouble is best avoided by:

(a) buying of certified stock.

(b) spraying the bushes regularly against 'big bud'.

(c) seeking expert advice where performance of bushes, particularly cropping, is falling off.

10 · Red and White Currants

Less popular by far than the blackcurrant in Britain, red and white currants are nonetheless a very useful fruit in their own right. On the Continent and in the U.S.A. on the other hand they far outshadow blackcurrants in popularity and importance. They possess a refreshingly different flavour which comes into its own in the form of red currant jelly and which combines excellently with a number of other fruits in the making of preserves. The white forms are particularly rich in flavour and in bygone days were considered a fine dessert – freshly picked strigs of fruit with bowls of cream and sugar being the recipe. Even without the two latter ingredients there are many who would agree just how refreshing a strig or two of white currants can be on a hot day.

Red and white currants are capable of producing very heavy crops, and providing site and soil are suitable and the bushes do not fall victim to winter bird damage (see p. 130) such results should be obtained without much difficulty. Moreover, these fruits, in common with gooseberries, lend themselves to numerous trained forms which can be invaluable where space is limited. Such trained specimens, usually in cordon or fan-trained form, are easy to protect from birds, particularly on walls and fences. Trained red and white currants are summarized later on p.127. In general, however, ordinary bushes are grown and the account immediately following is mainly concerned with those.

Site

Freedom from frost and cold winds are the primary requirements. The danger from spring frosts has already been fully discussed in Chapter 2. What may escape the unsuspecting is the damage that wind can cause in late spring on certain young fruit plants, not least the red currant. The danger period is late May and early June, when, if bushes are open to the full force of the wind, many of the finest shoots will be broken off and left hanging by the 'heel'. Quite often it can take two or three years longer than normal to shape and build up a bush because of this kind of trouble. Such instances are of course an exception and under average conditions there should be no difficulty.

Red and white currants are useful subjects for north-facing or other sun-starved walls and fences, but these must obviously be sufficiently protected to produce good results. Partial shade in the open garden is quite acceptable, though not preferable to a position in full sun.

Soil

The vast majority of soils will suffice, the least favourable being heavy soils that lie wet. Red and white currants are less tolerant of excessive wetness than blackcurrants and in particular resent such adverse conditions immediately after planting. Lighter loams adequately fed will probably produce the finest and heaviest crops; sandy soils can also give good results, but losses through dieback (see p. 131) will be much more numerous unless bushes are fed regularly and well. Chalk soils too require adequate humus if they are to provide good growth and cropping. Lime-induced chlorosis is not usually a major problem, particularly where manuring is generous.

Potash is the red and white currant's main requirement, in conjunction with adequate nitrogen. Many soils are deficient in both of these vital nutrients and they should be added (see p. 125).

Preparation of Ground

If the same course is followed as that outlined for blackcurrants on p. 102 this should be more than adequate. However, red currants are not such gross feeders, so that where both crops are being planted and manure or compost are in short supply blackcurrants should have first preference. The need for really clean ground is as important as for any other soft fruit.

Source of Planting Material

Although there is no certification scheme in operation for red and white currants it is still important to obtain young stock from a reliable source. Virus diseases *are* known to exist among red currants and workers at East Malling Research Station are in the process of producing healthy selections. The comparative un-importance of the crop commercially, however, has so far rendered any certification scheme unwarranted.

Planting

The autumn is preferable, but any of the winter months, up to and including February, are acceptable providing soil conditions and weather are right. Red currants are particularly intolerant of excessive wetness at time of planting. March planting is too late for comfort, since growth frequently starts during that month.

Unlike blackcurrants, red currant bushes are grown with a stem or 'leg' and it is important to give this good clearance above soil level. Only in this way can a tidy bush be kept in later years, avoiding the nuisance of suckers arising from the base of branches partially submerged by successive mulches. Like blackcurrants, the two-year-old bush is the most satisfactory for new planting.

N.B.: On some of the drier, poorer soils red and white currant bushes can be difficult to grow because of frequent losses through dieback (see p. 131). In such instances there may well be a case for growing them on the stool method, as for blackcurrants (see p. 104). In this way there is no vulnerable stem or leg, disease in which usually means the loss of the whole bush, and a constant supply of young branches is assured. Needless to say regular thinning is necessary and if a normal bush can be grown it is easier to manage.

Planting distances for garden culture are usually 5–6 ft apart each way.

Pruning after Planting

This is just as important as for the blackcurrant, possibly more so. If no pruning is done hardly any new growth develops and bushes can remain little more than planting size for years through neglect of pruning and feeding. The result is usually a paltry pound or so of inferior fruit instead of 12–15 lb. of fine currants per bush. The time of pruning for the newly planted bush can be an important factor where bird damage to buds is serious. In such cases it should be delayed until as late as possible so long as it is completed by the time the buds burst. Where bird damage is no problem any time following leaf-fall will be in order. In any event the netting of bushes is a sound move as soon as first signs of bird damage occur (see p. 124), for a whole crop can be lost in a very short time.

34. A one-year-old red currant, unpruned.
35. The same bush pruned.

36. A two-year-old red currant, unpruned.
37. The same bush pruned.

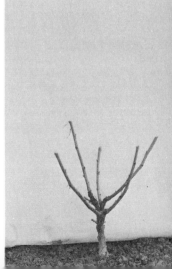

Pruning Details

The habit of fruiting of red and white currants is completely different from that of the blackcurrant. Red and white cultivars should develop a mass of fruiting spurs on the branches which will produce a generous quota of fruit buds with amazing regularity (pl. 38, p. 124). Thus a miniature tree can be formed, the same branches producing the crop year after year. This can be achieved however only with correct and regular pruning.

The pruning details are more or less rule of thumb. Cuts must always be made just above the selected bud to avoid leaving snags which may lead to dieback:

ONE-YEAR-OLD BUSH. This should consist of about three strong shoots. These are cut back hard to an *outward*-facing bud no more than three or four buds from the base. Any weak or badly placed shoots are removed completely (Pls. 34, 35,).

TWO-YEAR-OLD BUSH. Five to eight strong shoots should now be evident. They should be cut back to leave one-third their length, again to an outward-facing bud. In the process adequate and regular spacing should be aimed at, and badly placed or crowded shoots removed. Any smaller sides shoots should be shortened to one bud from the base (Pls. 36, 37).

THREE-YEAR-OLD BUSH. By now there should be numerous sturdy growths. Firstly shorten to one bud all weaker shoots. Next remove any unwanted stronger shoots completely. This should leave about eight or nine main shoots, which will be the permanent branches of the bush. These should be shortened by about half (but not more than half) their length to an outward-pointing bud. By choosing such buds, growth is directed *outwards* and an open-centred bush is produced to allow maximum sun and air and to facilitate picking.

FOURTH-YEAR ONWARDS. Side shoots will become increasingly numerous (except where bird damage has removed buds) and these are shortened hard back to a bud within an inch or so of the main branch (Pl. 38). This accounts for most of the bush and should leave only the branch leaders (i.e. the topmost shoots extending the branches themselves), which are tip-pruned by removing a quarter or so of their length.

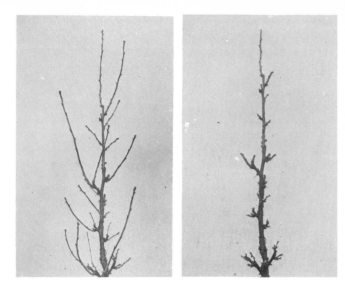

38 (*Left*) A branch of red currant, unpruned. (*Right*) the same bush pruned.

As bushes become older it may be advisable to replace worn-out branches and to do this use should be made of strong young shoots that frequently develop on the lower half of the bush. Where such growths are not required it is probably best to remove them completely rather than spur them back.

Summer Pruning

This is not essential on bushes but should be routine treatment for trained forms. Side shoots are shortened to five leaves (i.e. five leaves beyond the point at which new growth commenced) during the latter half of June. Branch leaders are *not* summer-pruned but are shortened in winter, when the side shoots should also be shortened to the standard spur system of one inch.

It is important to reserve summer pruning for bushes, etc. in full health and vigour – if growth is in any way lacking hold over summer treatment until it is restored.

Protection from Birds

Birds may leave a token offering of fruit on unprotected black-currants, but red and white currants will invariably be stripped completely. Netting must be done before fruits begin colouring, and at the same time some form of support, such as a central stake, to which any very heavily laden branches can be tied, should be applied.

Picking

Red currants, with their fine individual bunches, are much easier to pick than blackcurrants. Fruit should be picked in whole strigs or bunches, not individually, and should be gathered firm ripe and dry. Scissors are often preferred to thumb and forefinger, particularly on cultivars where the fruit is lying close to the branch. Over-ripe fruit will quickly go mouldy, even on the bush, in wet conditions.

Manuring

If possible well-decayed farmyard manure should be applied regularly in late April, once the soil has warmed. On good soils this should suffice but on soils known to be deficient in potash sulphate of potash should be given as well – an application of $\frac{1}{2}$ to $\frac{3}{4}$ oz. per sq. yd annually in February. Muriate of potash and Kainit should *not* be used since red and white currants are injured by their chloride content.

Where manure is not available apply sulphate of ammonia in February at 1 oz. per sq. yd. On very acid soils use Nitro Chalk or Nitra Shell instead at the same rate. Growth must not be excessive however, and where necessary nitrogenous fertilizers and mulching should be withheld for a year or so.

Phosphates are usually in adequate natural supply on most soils but every few years a sprinkling, say 3 oz. per sq. yd, of bone meal or superphosphate can be given.

Watering

Any soft fruit will benefit from timely watering and red and white currants are no exception. However, they are not so dependent on it as blackcurrants, where a maximum supply of new wood is essential, being the potential crop for the following year.

Weeding

The control of weeds is as important as for any other crop, and in general the remarks for blackcurrants on p. 109 apply equally here. A regular mulch on clean ground will do much to alleviate the weed problem.

Cultivars

The number of cultivars on offer in fruit nursery catalogues has dwindled and frequently not more than one or two are listed. Nevertheless the following are still available from one source or another.

Those most widely grown are marked *.

A. *RED*

EARLIEST OF FOURLANDS: First early, heavy-cropper and the vigorous growth demands plenty of space.

*LAXTON'S NO. 1. Early, very widely planted and very heavy and reliable cropper. A neat well-shaped bush is easily obtained.

FAY'S PROLIFIC. Early. Very attractive, large, scarlet fruits, but the habit of producing shoots that fail to produce spurs and side shoots has caused this currant to fall from popularity.

LAXTON'S PERFECTION. Mid-season. A fine fruit where good bushes can be grown but a tendency to produce bare or blind shoots plus its susceptibility to the blowing-out of shoots in windy weather has prevented this cultivar becoming well established.

*RED LAKE. Mid to late mid-season. One of the finest introductions to be made and now probably the leading red currant. A heavy-cropper producing long strigs of large deep-red berries. Raised in U.S.A.

RABY CASTLE. Late mid-season; much planted at one time but now largely superseded. Not renowned for heavy cropping. Berries medium-sized.

RIVERS' LATE RED (syn. PRINCE ALBERT). Late. A very useful currant because of its lateness. Not a heavy-cropper and tends to take rather longer to start fruiting on young bushes than most.

*WILSON'S LONG BUNCH. Very late. Probably the most popular late cultivar owing to its reliability in producing good crops of medium-sized fruit. Mixed stocks exist and a reliable source is necessary if the true cultivar is to be obtained.

N.B.: Two newly-introduced continental red currants may in time become available. These are 'Jonkheer van Tets' (very early) and 'Rondom' (late).

B. *WHITE*

Confusion among named cultivars is suspected and what one nurseryman may offer under a particular name might appear under another elsewhere. The following are worth noting:

WHITE DUTCH. Very pale, milky white.

WHITE GRAPE. Good quality, heavy cropper, not widely listed.

WHITE TRANSPARENT. Often listed but more acid than most.

WHITE VERSAILLES. Probably the sweetest of the white currants and well worth growing.

Trained Forms of Red and White Currant

These are well worth considering where space is limited – they normally give particularly fine samples of fruit.

Site

Although sunny walls may be used, the more shady ones, even those facing north, will produce excellent crops providing there is shelter from cold winds at flowering time. Low fences, open trellis work and other forms of support may also be used, but whatever the position adequate wires for training will be needed at about 6–9 ins. intervals.

Soil

Details generally are as given on p. 120. Beware however of the poor soil that is so often left adjacent to house and other walls. This combined with the footings of the wall frequently leads to impoverished growth and poor cropping unless adequate preparation and after-care is given.

Planting

Details generally as on p. 121. The stem should be placed 6 ins. away from the wall and no tying to wires or stakes should be done until the plant has had a chance to settle. Two-year-old specimens are the most satisfactory.

Pruning

(A) CORDONS. These may take one of a number of forms – single, double or triple cordons or double 'U'. The first two are probably the best for ease of training, etc. But no matter which type is grown the principles of pruning are the same – basically summer pruning, plus the shortening of the leading shoot in winter, together with any tidying-up required. The summer treatment is best done about mid-June just before the fruit begins to colour. All side shoots are cut back to four leaves. In winter shorten the leading shoot or shoots by one third of the length of the new growth made, leaving a *maximum* of 9–10 ins. of new wood; also reduce the summer-pruned side shoots to one or two buds. Once a cordon has reached the desired height the leading shoot can if necessary be included in the summer treatment.

Occasionally rank sucker-like shoots are thrown up from near the base of the cordon. These are obvious from an early stage and should be *broken off* cleanly at the point of origin when still young and soft.

(B) FAN. This form is rather more exacting than a simple cordon but once formed the pruning is precisely the same as outlined in (A) above. The only difference is that instead of having just one or two leading shoots there may be a dozen or more.

Training

Cordons, and possibly fans also, are available from some specialist fruit nurseries. However, where cuttings (see p. 120) are available from *healthy* bushes it is fascinating to train one's own. Details, briefly, are as follows:

(a) *Single Cordon*. Train the topmost growth from the rooted cutting to a bamboo. Initially, pinch back any other shoots to two or three leaves, removing them completely once the main shoot has been established. This is the treatment for the first growing season. Thereafter prune as described for cordons above.

(b) *Double or 'U' cordon*. Train the top *two* growths from the rooted cutting to bamboos placed at 30° to the ground. When the shoots are about 3 ins. long allow them to grow vertically to form the 'U', thus making the branches about 6 ins. apart. Remove other shoots as for (a). Thereafter prune as above.

(c) *Triple cordon* (Pl. 48, p. 144) – train the top growth from the cutting vertically and the next two available shoots below as for a 'U' cordon. The three shoots should be spaced about 6 ins. apart. To be successful in this initial stage it is important to choose a strong cutting that is developing three or more shoots of adequate and comparable vigour. After the first growing season from a cutting, prune as under cordons on p. 128.

(d) *Double 'U' cordon* – Stage one is to train a 'U' cordon as described under (b) above, but with the branches 12–14 ins. apart. The two branches are then pruned the following winter to points just above the beginning of the vertical growth on each side. Good strong shoots should develop from the hard pruning and on each side two are chosen to form another 'U', thus forming a double 'U'. If the initial spacing of 12–14 ins. between the first 'arms' is observed the four permanent branches should automatically develop at about 6 ins. apart.

N.B.: Sometimes better 'U' and triple cordons may be obtained by using good one-year-old plants and pruning them back to two or three buds on each shoot in winter. Stronger growth may then result than might be obtained from some cuttings in their first year, thus giving a greater choice of good shoots for training.

Manuring and other cultural details – as for bush forms.

Pests

APHIDS (greenfly). There are several species of aphids, including the rather spectacular red currant blister aphid, which causes the corrugated red blisters sometimes seen on young leaves in late spring or early summer.

Control. Tar-oil wash in December to January to kill over-wintering eggs, or malathion during the growing season as soon as the pest is seen.

CAPSIDS. This pest can be very troublesome, feeding as it does by rupturing the tissues of the young leaves (Pl. 31, p. 114). Normal growth is rendered impossible, the leaf becomes corrugated with rusty spots where damage has occurred. In bad infestations the spots may join together to form large holes.

Control. DDT spray at grape-bud stage (i.e. when unopened flower trusses resemble miniature bunches of grapes, see Pl. 32, p. 114).

39. Bird damage on a dormant red currant. Gooseberry is similarly affected. (*Left*) Normal growth. (*Right*) Bare branch due to successive winters of bird damage.

BIRDS. Damage varies according to site, locality and season. Bare lengths of branch (Pl. 39) that should normally be covered with fruiting spurs are a sure sign of bird damage, usually by bullfinches but often also by tits and sparrows.

Control. Net over as necessary, giving supports sufficient to withstand snowfall. The nets should be removed before the flowers open.

GOOSEBERRY SAWFLY. This pest occurs spasmodically, but a wary eye should be kept from the time flowering finishes, which is usually about mid-May. Devastating defoliation can occur in a few days (Pl. 49, p. 146). The caterpillars, green and black in colour, feed voraciously. Initially, they usually concentrate on the centre or underside of the bush and damage may not be easily noticed.

Control. Spray with derris or malathion at the first sign of damage. Repeat the treatment fourteen days later if necessary.

N.B.: Big bud mite, or blackcurrant gall mite, is of little or no consequence on red currants. It can occur, but infected buds shrivel and drop.

Diseases (other than Virus Diseases)

Fortunately there are few serious diseases of red and white currants, but the two mentioned below can be troublesome, particularly on lighter, poorer soils.

DIEBACK. Shoots suddenly shrivel and die, often with the crop three-parts developed. The trouble is caused by grey mould (botrytis) fungus which has gained entry through a pruning wound or some other lesion.

Control. Cut back immediately to *completely clean wood.* Keep the bush open to avoid excessive humidity and, where the disease is troublesome, paint larger pruning wounds with a bituminous tree paint. Where infection reaches the main stem the bush is as good as lost (unless grown on the stool principle, where 'sucker' shoots will quickly act as replacements; see p. 104).

CORAL SPOT. This disease causes branches to wilt and shrivel during spring and summer, after which masses of small red spots appear on the infected area.

Control. Entry, as with botrytis, is via dead pruning snags and other wounds. Such snags should be avoided when pruning and it is advisable to paint over larger pruning cuts to seal them. Wilting branches must be removed immediately, cutting back to a point where the wood is completely healthy.

Virus Diseases

Certain virus diseases have been identified in red currants. The symptoms are not easy for the untrained eye to detect, however. Sensible precautions would include (a) buying the bushes from a specialist grower and (b) dispensing with any that fail to grow and/or crop satisfactorily.

11 · Gooseberries

The gooseberry is a native plant of much of Europe and northern Asia, including the British Isles. It has been widely cultivated here since the sixteenth century, and it is said to have first come into prominence during the reign of Henry VIII. It is the first fruit of the season and for best value the fruits should be allowed to swell near to full size and then be used green for jamming, bottling, etc. There is, in fact, probably no more successful fruit than the gooseberry for bottling. Ripe dessert gooseberries are now quite a luxury and seldom seen in the shops.

With a little attention to pruning, manuring and spraying, three or four gooseberry bushes should be capable of supplying the average household with more than sufficient fruit in most seasons.

Site

Provided there is adequate protection from wind and frost gooseberries should succeed in most gardens. Partial shade is quite acceptable – though not preferable. As much use can be made of walls and fences as for redcurrants (see p. 120), which means that these two fruits are particularly useful where space is strictly limited.

It is important that the site should be well drained. Gooseberries will not tolerate waterlogged ground and are among the first subjects to be affected by such conditions.

Soil

The primary requirements are a cool, moist, yet well-drained root run together with adequate potash. Many sandy soils will need special attention in this respect. Gooseberries and redcurrants have much in common in their general cultivation needs, and these two crops should be grouped together in any planting plan (Pl. 1, p. 11).

The performance of gooseberries fluctuates widely depending on local soil conditions and some cultivars are much better than others for particular soil types. For example, 'Whinham's Industry' is usually more reliable than most on heavy soils, which are generally unsatisfactory for gooseberries; 'Lancer' is a safe recommendation for lighter ground, while 'Leveller', which is so highly prized as a dessert fruit when fully ripe, is particularly intolerant of too heavy or too light soils.

Chalk soils should have plentiful dressings of humus before and after planting and, although results will vary, gooseberries are usually more tolerant of such conditions than most fruits.

Preparation for Planting

This needs to be thorough. Gooseberries fruit on young wood as well as old, so that good annual growth is called for, and this cannot be guaranteed unless the ground is in good condition. Preferably use a plot that has already been well worked and prepared for several seasons; prepare it early in the autumn and dig in good quantities of rotted farmyard manure and compost, peat or leafmould. It is important that any peat should be evenly moist *before* it is used. Areas that have been less well worked should be double dug. Planting should not be started until the ground is completely clean of weeds.

Source of Material

Young gooseberry bushes are more difficult to raise than black-currants or redcurrants. Cuttings do not root so readily and even the successful ones sometimes refuse to make adequate growth. The responsible nursery will ensure that strong young bushes are supplied that have been raised from carefully selected stock bushes renowned for healthy vigour and cropping. Even with a fruit as unglamorous as the gooseberry a reliable source of supply counts for a lot.

Planting

There is no doubt that autumn planting gives markedly better results than winter or early spring planting. The gooseberry is particularly early in moving into growth, so autumn-planted bushes will have an obvious advantage: growth is stronger and first crops are that much heavier in consequence.

There is a second point to watch for. Gooseberry bushes need to be grown on a distinct 'leg' or stem to give good clearance from the ground. To meet this requirement, it may be necessary

133

to trim off a few of the topmost roots and plant the bush a little *higher* than the nursery soil mark. This is also an insurance against suckering, which can be a problem with older bushes (Pl. 63, p. 177).

Planting distances should be 6 ft × 5 ft at least – rather more if possible, particularly where soil fertility is known to be high. The distances should be varied to suit the growth habit of individual cultivars where this is known, e.g. 6 ft × 5 ft for 'Leveller' or 'Whitesmith', but up to 5 ft × 8 ft for vigorous growers like 'Whinham's Industry'. Certainly if several rows are to be planted a *minimum* of 8 ft between rows should be allowed to facilitate picking and general cultivation.

Pruning after Planting

This is particularly important. Bushes can soon lose their shape under weight of early crops and the aim during the first three years or so must be to develop a framework of strong, well-spaced, *upward-growing* branches. Many cultivars have a drooping habit of growth (Pls. 40, 41; 46, 47, pp. 136, 139) and unless adequate shaping is done in the early stages a shapely free-cropping bush will not be obtained.

Time of Pruning

Winter pruning can be done from leaf fall onwards. However, bullfinches, sparrows and other birds can devastate bushes by feeding on the overwintering buds. Ideally, bushes should be netted throughout the winter where experience shows that damage is likely to occur. If they are not, then pruning should be delayed until March (or even later). This helps in a twofold way. Firstly, a tangled thorny bush can present more of a problem for a bird than a pruned one with well-spaced branches; secondly, the damaged shoots can be pruned out and those with a good or full complement of buds retained. In fact it is quite possible (though not the best practice) to delay pruning until the first leaves have unfolded, by which time it is abundantly clear which are the damaged shoots.

Pruning Details

The following pruning treatment should be followed:

ONE-YEAR-OLD BUSH. A good specimen should consist of three good shoots, sometimes four. These must be shortened to about

134

a quarter of their length, which usually means cutting to leave three to four buds at the base (Pls. 40, 41). Where shoots are spreading rather than upright, an *upward*-pointing bud should be chosen above which the cut should be made; this will ensure reasonably upright growth the following year.

TWO-YEAR-OLD BUSH. A good bush will have six to eight good shoots plus some weaker ones. The latter are pruned back to one or two buds (about 1 in.) to form fruiting spurs. The main shoots are then shortened, by half their length if growth is strong, perhaps by two-thirds if it appears at all weak. At this stage shaping the framework is still all-important and if weaker bushes are not pruned hard enough strong branches are less likely to result. Any spreading tendency is corrected as described under one-year-old bush above.

THREE-YEAR-OLD BUSH (Pls. 42, 43). Many more side shoots should now be seen. These must be shortened – up to 3 ins. for stronger shoots and down to 1 in. for smaller ones. Very weak shoots must be cut out completely, in company with any stronger shoots that are either surplus to requirements or growing in an awkward position (such as across the centre of the bush, or downwards). Having thinned out and shortened side shoots it only remains to shorten the branch leaders. These are cut to about half their length.

PRUNING IN SUBSEQUENT YEARS. This follows the pattern set out under three-year-olds. In particular, young wood must always be encouraged, using it in older bushes to replace worn-out pieces or branches. The centres of bushes must be open and branches kept well spaced and well clear of the ground to facilitate picking (Pls. 44, 45). When vigour tends to fall off after a year or two of heavy cropping, branch leaders can be cut by rather *more* than half their length. This coupled with sensible feeding should induce stronger growth.

It will be found that branches tend to arch over in succession, partly with the weight of the fruit and partly because of the natural drooping habit of some cultivars, as already mentioned (Pls. 46, 47). It is important continually to select new branch leaders as required, and having cut back to them, to prune them quite hard to induce growth from them rather than fruit.

40. One-year-old gooseberries with (*left*) drooping and (*right*) upright growth – unpruned.

41. The same bushes pruned. With drooping growth (*left*) it is important to prune to an upward-pointing bud.

42. A three-year-old gooseberry, unpruned.

43. The same bush pruned.

44. A fully grown gooseberry of upright habit, unpruned.

45. The same bush pruned.

46. A fully grown gooseberry of drooping habit, unpruned for two seasons.

47. The same bush pruned.

SUMMER PRUNING. Summer pruning as such is not essential for bush gooseberries, although it is very necessary for trained cordons, etc. (see p. 143). In spite of this there are circumstances where tipping of the shoots during the summer is desirable. This is where an outbreak of the disease American gooseberry mildew occurs. The tips of young shoots are affected (see Pl. 50, p. 147) and if the diseased wood remains it will release spores of the disease later in the summer and autumn to carry the disease over to the next season. Thus, if the top third of every shoot is removed and the prunings are burnt, a sensible step has been taken towards controlling the trouble. This disease, if not kept in check, can be devastating (see p. 148). Tipping should be done in July and by mid-August at the latest.

PRUNING AFTER SEVERE BIRD DAMAGE. Once a branch has been badly denuded of buds any existing spurs will tend to die out, and the only way to put matters right is to prune hard back to a point where a strong bud is evident. The resultant new growth is then used to rebuild the branch.

Protection from Birds

Bird damage to gooseberries is usually a less serious problem than with other soft fruits, particularly where the fruit is picked green. However, if ripe dessert berries are desired, protection will most certainly be required. The overwintering buds normally need protection, as indicated in the foregoing paragraphs, and every effort should be made to net the bushes where necessary (see also p. 130).

Picking

A first early sample of half-grown fruits is liked by many – the first fresh fruit of the new season. This serves more than one purpose for, in thinning the crop, it leads to larger fruits for later pickings, particularly where the crop is a heavy one. Gooseberries retained for use as ripe dessert specimens should for true flavour be picked while warm from the sun.

Watering

Watering can play an important role in dry spells, for without it growth may be checked and in severe heat the foliage and fruits scorched, especially on hot sandy soils. At least the equivalent of 1 in. of rain should be given at a time, that is $4\frac{1}{2}$ gallons per square yd (for the calculation of this see p. 23). From mid-May to mid-July is the crucial time.

Weeding

This is important and the remarks under blackcurrants (p.109) apply equally here. Do not dig between bushes – it does far more harm than good because of damage to the roots.

Manuring

Adequate supplies of potash are important, since the gooseberry, like the apple and red currant, is soon affected by a deficiency of it (see p. 42). An average annual dressing should be $\frac{1}{2}$ to $\frac{3}{4}$ oz. per sq. yd of sulphate of potash. Too much should not be applied. The deficiency is usually more marked on poorer, sandy soils, causing premature leaf fall and, in consequence, a general weakening of the bush.

Nitrogen is equally important to encourage good growth for heavy crops. It should not be overdone, however, as this increases the risk of shoots being broken by wind. Surface mulches of dung and compost in spring give the best results, because they reduce any soil moisture deficit as well as providing a weak general feed.

Phosphates are comparatively unimportant – an occasional 3–4 oz. dressing per sq. yd of superphosphate should suffice.

Cultivars

Reference to older catalogues and reference books will reveal a host of sorts to choose from. The names are fascinating and one is left wondering what lay behind the christening of such cultivars as 'Dan's Mistake', 'Broom Girl', 'Crown Bob', 'Ironmonger', 'Slaughterman', 'Pretty Boy' and 'Tally Ho'! The gooseberry names are in a class of their own, and undoubtedly originated in the rivalry and gamesmanship of the old gooseberry clubs.

Here is a select list of some gooseberries that are fairly easy to obtain. These are, in alphabetical order:

BROOM GIRL. Early, ripens yellow. Very large, round fruit; excellent for dessert purposes. Bush vigorous and growth fairly upright.

CARELESS. Mid-season; ripens whitish yellow. Distinctly long and oval in shape and excellent for bottling and preserves. Bush moderately vigorous, spreading. Widely grown.

EARLY SULPHUR (syn. GOLDENBALL). Early. Ripens golden yellow. Medium–small, round, hairy and possessing excellent flavour. Growth at first upright then spreading.

GOLDEN DROP. Mid-season, ripens golden yellow. Small round downy fruits of good flavour. Growth moderate and bush tidy in habit.

KEEPSAKE. Second early, ripens to pale green. Medium to large oval hairy fruit, and of very good quality and flavour. Rather prone to mildew and frost damage. Bush vigorous and spreading.

LANCASHIRE LAD. Mid-season, ripens deep red. Large oval hairy fruit. Flavour fair only. Very resistant to mildew. Not suited to poor soils where growth may be stunted; otherwise vigorous rather spreading and a heavy cropper.

LANGLEY GAGE. Mid-season, ripens pale whitish-green. Rather small round-oval fruit, smooth and transparent and of superb flavour. Bush vigorous and growth upright.

LANCER (= HOWARD'S LANCER). Late, ripens greenish yellow. Large smooth round-oval fruits of fine flavour. A fine gooseberry and excellent for bottling, etc. as well as for dessert. Bush vigorous and spreading.

LEVELLER. Mid-season, ripens yellow. Large round-oval fruits, almost smooth and of excellent flavour. The most widely grown dessert gooseberry. Bush moderately vigorous and spreading; rather fastidious as to soil conditions, which must be good.

MAY DUKE. Early, ripens red. Medium-sized round fruits, almost smooth, excellent cooked or preserved, moderate dessert only. Bush moderately vigorous; fairly upright. Valuable for early crops.

WHINHAM'S INDUSTRY. Mid-season, ripens red. Fairly large oval fruits, hairy, and sweetly flavoured when ripe. Bush vigorous at first upright, becoming spreading with cropping. One of the finest gooseberries, doing well on most soils but subject to mildew.

WHITESMITH. Second early, ripens pale yellowish-white; medium to large oval fruits, downy and of fine flavour. Bush moderately vigorous at first then spreading. A very good gooseberry.

The following are occasionally listed and are worthy of a trial in any garden:

BEDFORD RED. Mid-season, ripening dull red. Bush upright.

CHAMPAGNE YELLOW. Late, ripening yellow and very sweet. Bush upright.

COUSEN'S SEEDLING. Very late, ripening yellow. Bush spreading and growth rather weak.

CROWN BOB. Mid-season, ripening red. Bush spreading and vigorous.

DAN'S MISTAKE. Mid-season, ripening pale red. Bush spreading and growth rather weak.

GREEN GEM. Late, ripening green. Bush upright and compact. A very valuable gooseberry but for reasons unknown is seldom listed.

GUNNER. Late mid-season ripening, yellowish green. Bush spreading.

KING OF TRUMPS. Very late ripening, pale green. Bush spreading and growth moderate only.

LONDON. Late, ripening dark red. Bush spreading, growth vigorous.

LORD DERBY. Late, ripening dark red. Bush spreading, growth weak.

PROFIT. Mid-season, ripening green. Bush spreading.

TELEGRAPH. Late, ripening green. Bush spreading, growth weak.

WARRINGTON. Late ripening, pale red. Bush spreading, growth vigorous.

WHITE LION. Late ripening, white. Bush spreading, growth vigorous.

Trained Forms of Gooseberry

Details quoted under red currants on pp. 127–9 apply to gooseberries also, except that the laterals need not be shortened quite so severely in winter. Some of the finest gooseberries are grown on trained cordons (Pl. 48) and fans, but feeding and pruning must be attended to regularly for good results. In the summer pruning of trained gooseberries some authorities prefer to pinch out the growing tips of the shoots with finger and thumb when 5 ins. or so in length.

48. A gooseberry triple cordon.

Standard Gooseberries

Seldom seen here, standard gooseberries are quite common in Germany and imported samples from that country can occasionally be found. The selected cultivar is grafted onto a rootstock, usually *Ribes aureum*, which also forms the stem. The standard would seem to have obvious advantages for picking and pruning.

Pests

APHIDS (greenfly). Several species infest gooseberries and can seriously affect growth if not kept under control.

Control. Tar-oil winter wash annually, unless gooseberry red spider is troublesome, in which case use DNOC. Should infestation occur in spring or summer in spite of a winter wash, spray with dimethoate (allow seven days between spraying and picking) or malathion.

BIRDS. See under red currant, p. 130. (The serious damage is that caused by the wholesale pecking out of overwintering buds.)

CAPSIDS. Occasionally damage can reach serious proportions. This is when so much of the leaf tissue has been ruptured that normal growth is impossible. The same pest affects black, red and white currants (see Pl. 31, p. 114).

Control. Spray with DDT immediately after blossoming if the pest is expected to cause serious damage.

GOOSEBERRY RED SPIDER MITE (=BRYOBIA MITE). Not widely troublesome but should be controlled when seen. Foliage is bronzed by the sucking of the mites and drops prematurely.

Control. By spraying with dimethoate or malathion. DNOC winter wash will kill any over-wintering eggs.

GOOSEBERRY SAWFLY. It is the caterpillar stage in the life cycle of this sawfly that causes the damage. The caterpillars are olive green and black in colour and usually congregate at first in the middle or on the underside of bushes. Bushes can quickly be defoliated (Pl. 49). They appear from about mid-May and also cause damage on red and white currants.

49. Gooseberry sawfly. (*Left*) Damage on a gooseberry shoot. (*Right*)
An undamaged shoot.

50. American gooseberry mildew, infected shoot tips. White powdery areas also develop on leaves and in severe cases on the fruit as well.

51. Leaf spot disease on a gooseberry leaf. Blackcurrants are similarly affected.

Control. Spray with derris or malathion at the first sign of damage. Repeat the application fourteen days later if necessary.

Diseases

AMERICAN GOOSEBERRY MILDEW. Quite the worst of all troubles among gooseberries, it spread from the U.S.A. during the early 1900s. White powdery areas appear on leaves of young shoots and fruits, later turning brown and of a felt-like consistency. The young shoot tips are usually the first area to show signs of trouble (Pl. 50).

Control. Prevention is better than cure and two or three sprays of ordinary washing soda from March onwards will often be sufficient. Use $\frac{1}{2}$ lb. washing soda in $2\frac{1}{2}$ gallons water plus a spreader. Where mildew is really troublesome regular spraying with dinocap may be necessary, but whatever material is used an early start with spraying is the answer, the first spray just before flowering, the next soon after the fruit sets and thereafter at fourteen-day intervals if necessary. Lime sulphur can be used and is very effective, but yellow-fruited cultivars such as 'Leveller' and 'Golden Drop' are intolerant and should not be sprayed with it. Normal strength of use is $\frac{1}{2}$ pint lime sulphur in $2\frac{1}{2}$ gallons of water, but only $\frac{1}{4}$ pint to $2\frac{1}{2}$ gallons of water after fruit has set. Lime sulphur must not be used on fruit destined for canning.

Mention has already been made of infected young shoots, and their removal before mid-August will assist in checking the disease. The prunings should of course be burnt.

BOTRYTIS. This disease can be serious where soil is poor and growth is not as vigorous as it should be. Bushes usually die back branch by branch and once the main stem is infected the whole bush is lost.

Control. Cut out shoots and branches well behind the infected part to a point where the wood is completely clean and healthy. Dead branches and bushes must be burnt and wounds are best painted over with a fungicidal wound paint.

LEAF SPOT. This is the same disease as that which affects black-currants. It is not usually as severe on gooseberry (Pl. 51). For full details and control measures see p. 116.

12 · Blueberries

Much confusion exists over the use of such names as blueberries, bilberries, blaeberries, cranberries, huckleberries and whortleberries. The named cultivars of blueberries now available and with which this account is mainly concerned are derived from *Vaccinium corymbosum*. They are known in their native U.S.A. as Highbush Blueberries and their fruits are considerably larger than our wild bilberries. Bilberry, blaeberry, huckleberry and whortleberry are in fact local names for one and the same plant native to many moorland parts of Britain, the small blue-fruited *Vaccinium myrtillus*, growing 9–18 ins. high.

The cranberry, *Vaccinium oxycoccus* (*Oxycoccus palustris*) has deep red, roundish fruits, considerably larger than bilberries, and thrives in moist, peaty, almost boggy conditions. Huckleberry is also the common name given to the fruit of several species of *Gaylussacia* native to eastern North America which are closely allied to the Vacciniums. All these various plants have one thing in common – they grow on acid moorland soils.

Quite recently confusion over these names has been highlighted by the appearance at prominent fruit competitions of fairly large, shiny, jet-black fruits, under the name of 'huckleberry' – sometimes the diameter of a thumbnail in size. These in fact are the 'garden huckleberry', a species akin to our native *Solanum nigrum*, which is a common weed of many cultivated areas and produces similar but smaller fruits. It is considered that the fruits of some forms of *S. nigrum* are, to a certain extent, poisonous if eaten in large quantities; whether or not the fruits of the garden huckleberry possess the same properties has not been proven, but they are of little culinary value and it is probably wiser not to eat them. The garden huckleberry is often known as *S. guineense* or *S. intrusum*, but some confusion exists as to the correct botanical name. The large-fruited American cultivars of blueberry (Pl. 52, see also illustration on cover) are comparatively new to this country but have been a firm favourite in the United States for many years. Provided soil conditions are

52. American Highbush blueberries. A number of named cultivars are now available. See also illustration on cover.

suitable, this is an interesting new fruit, requiring little space, only a minimum of time in cultivation, and also providing good autumn colour. The fruit is excellent stewed or in pies, though it does not possess a particularly pronounced or strong flavour compared, for example, with blackcurrants. It may also be bottled or deep-frozen.

Site

An open, sunny place is preferable, with a cool, moist root run. Excessive moisture is harmful however, and the plant will quickly deteriorate in water-logged conditions.

Soil

This must be sufficiently acid. Generally speaking blueberries will thrive where rhododendrons and azaleas do, i.e. where the soil is acid and comparatively light. Heavier ground is unsatisfactory unless adequate quantities of peat and sand can be worked in to improve matters.

For distinctly alkaline soils (pH 7·0 and above) blueberries should not be considered, short of planting in tubs or specially excavated and lined beds. Without such precautions gradual seepage from surrounding ground will have adverse effects sooner

150

or later, although these can sometimes be offset by watering in sequestrene solutions. The acid common lands and moorlands of Surrey, Hampshire and parts of Dorset and Somerset are ideal for blueberries. This is worth noting because this poor type of soil is frequently unsuitable for good results with many garden crops.

Preparation for Planting

A good garden soil should need little if any added material, but some peat can be worked in if necessary. Newly broken common land on the other hand requires thorough digging with the incorporation of well-rotted manure or compost (providing it contains no lime or other alkaline substance such as mortar rubble) as well as peat. Prepare the ground well in advance of planting.

Planting

As usual, autumn planting is preferable, but up to and including March is acceptable. No manure should be used when planting, but a little moist peat worked around the roots is ideal. This will guard against any premature drying out in spring and will encourage quick rooting and establishment of the young plant. The young bushes can be planted at 6 ft apart and an inch or so deeper than the existing soil mark, on the same lines as for blackcurrants (see p. 104). In fact, cultivation details for blueberries are similar to those for blackcurrants in many respects.

Post-Planting Treatment

No pruning treatment is necessary. The all-important thing to guard against is dryness at the roots, and a mulch of peat or compost plus some water if a really dry spell sets in should meet this. The fact that acid soils suitable for blueberries are often dry sandy ones means that special care must be taken to keep the plants moist. Without adequate water, fruit size will suffer and there may be little or no new growth.

Firming the plants around the roots is important following any severe frosts.

Protection from Birds

The ripening fruits are a great attraction for blackbirds and thrushes and, like so many soft fruits, must be netted if the crop is to be saved. The blueberry is very accommodating because nets used for currants, strawberries, etc., will be free in August and September for ripening blueberries. Better still of course would be to include blueberries in the fruit cage.

Picking

Bushes will need to be picked over three or four times for the ripest fruits. The ripe fruits usually hang for a day or two so that, unlike some blackcurrants, the percentage of fallen fruit is unlikely to be serious. Blueberry pie is a favourite dish and well worth a trial on any menu. The earlier cultivars start ripening about mid-July.

Pruning

Regular annual pruning is *not* required. What is necessary is the removal of some of the oldest wood once the bushes have commenced cropping, always leaving any strong young wood intact.

Manuring

There should be an annual application of sulphate of ammonia at 1 oz. per sq. yd in March, although some authorities suggest $\frac{1}{2}$ oz. in April and a further similar dressing in July. Applications should be adjusted in the light of results obtained in individual gardens. A sprinkling of sulphate of potash at $\frac{1}{2}$ oz. per sq. yd each winter would also be wise, since acid sandy soils are usually deficient in this element. Superphosphate should be applied in alternate winters at 3 oz. per sq. yd.

Just as important as the fertilizer is an annual spring mulch of peat and/or compost. In particular composted sawdust is held to be excellent for the purpose.

Watering

Unless this is attended to as required results may well be disappointing. Adequate new growth is necessary each year – without it crops will soon fall off. Sufficient soil moisture is the best means of obtaining this growth.

Cultivars

Sources of supply in this country are strictly limited but certain cultivars are available, including 'Coville', 'Concord', 'Herbert' and 'Jersey'. There are also a number of others, but from the limited reports available in this country so far 'Jersey' seems to be one of the most reliable.

13 · Grapes Out-of-Doors

This short account of grape-growing in the open is simply concerned with vines trained on walls and fences, and not those grown in greenhouses or under cloches. The growing of grapes under vineyard techniques is quite another matter – a specialized subject in itself.*

Basically there are three key factors in the successful cultivation of grapes on outside walls and fences. These are (a) a cultivar suitable for the purpose, (b) correct and regular pruning and (c) suitable soil. Since all of these conditions should not be difficult to satisfy there is no reason why far more grapes should not be grown in this way. The following brief account gives the essential details, based on the old, time-honoured methods of the great private gardens. There are of course other systems and techniques but they would only confuse this simple account.

Site

A warm sunny wall or fence is essential. First it should be decided how the vine is to be trained. Wires should then be fixed at the required distances to carry the framework. The 'nails' known as vine-eyes are ideal for the purpose; it is a simple matter to thread the wire through the eye, while the length of the 'nail' is purposely designed to keep the wire an inch or two away from the wall.

Soil

The bed should be composed of reasonably good, well-drained garden soil, certainly not too rich or strong and preferably not too poor. If there is a choice, it is better to have poor rather than over-rich soil, since the latter only serves to encourage rank, soft growth that will fail to ripen and crop satisfactorily.

---

* Invaluable work has been done on viticulture by Mr Barrington Brock of Oxted in Surrey. Any readers deeply interested in vines and wines will find his booklets a mine of information. See also *The Cultivation of Apricots, Figs, Peaches, Nectarines and Grapes* by J. Wilson, Royal Horticultural Society, revised edition 1966.

Preparation for Planting

Except on the poorest soils all that is necessary is to fork over the area selected to a good depth. If the soil is really poor, either incorporate a little well-rotted manure or alternatively change one or two barrow-loads of it for some better material from elsewhere in the garden. Failing manure sprinkle on a little bone meal (say, 3 oz. per sq. yd) and rake in. The soil should be uniformly firm before planting is started.

Planting

Late autumn is the best time. Young vines are often supplied in pots. If so, water the plant well in the pot. Then carefully tap it out and spread its roots before setting it in a planting hole some 9–12 ins. away from the wall or fence. Plant firmly but do not tie the plant to any adjacent wires until it has had time to settle. A sprinkling of well-rotted compost can be spread around the plant if required; otherwise this is all that is necessary.

After a month or so the main shoot can be suitably tied to a wire or stake.

Time of Pruning

The time of pruning is important. This is because vines can bleed copiously through pruning wounds if the cuts are made at a time when they are not completely dormant. December is a safe month, January usually so but doubtful in the occasional very mild winter. Therefore December is the month to aim at.

Pruning Details (Single Rod)

It is important to do this correctly and regularly. Once initial training and shaping has been done the pruning is common to all forms of vine. A single rod (Pl. 54), cordon or stem is the simplest form of vine to grow, and this would be built up as follows:

FIRST SUMMER. Choose the strongest shoot as the leader or stem of the cordon and train it carefully to a bamboo. Pinch any side shoots back to 3 ft.

FIRST WINTER. Having allowed the vine to grow for the first season, cut back the main shoot to a point where the wood is

53. Winter pruning of vines, cutting side shoots to one, or at the most two, buds from the base in December.

54. A well-cared-for single-rod vine under glass. Note the evenly spaced lateral growths which will be controlled by pinching, as indicated (see text p. 156). Similar treatment should be given to vines on walls and fences in the open.

hard and fully ripened – even if this means cutting back to within 6 ins. of the ground. Laterals are pruned to one bud from their base.

SECOND SUMMER. The leading shoot is allowed to continue unrestricted. Any lateral shoots are allowed to grow to 2–3 ft and are then pinched at the tip. No fruit should be allowed and any flower trusses should be cut off.

SECOND WINTER. Laterals pinched during the summer are pruned hard back to one, or at the most two, buds from the base (Pl. 53).

The leader is shortened to a height of about 3 ft – or shorter if necessary where there is any doubt of wood being fully ripened. Unripe, soft wood is liable to winter killing and disease and it is never wise to retain any shoots in this category.

THIRD SUMMER. If the vine is growing well one or two bunches of grapes may now be taken. If it is not there is only one sensible answer – do not let the vine fruit. The leading shoot should be trained on as before. Laterals should now be stopped by pinching at 1 ft or, where a bunch of grapes is being taken, to two leaves beyond the bunch (Pl. 54). Sub-laterals will often develop from this stopping of vigorous laterals. These should have their tips pinched out by the first leaf.

THIRD WINTER. Laterals are treated as under 'second winter' and this winter treatment is now repeated year after year. Spurs may become gnarled and woody with the passage of time but should still produce their annual quota of vigorous fruiting shoots. Any overcrowded ones should be cut out completely (Pl. 55).

The leading shoot is now shortened to leave another 3 ft or so of new, ripened wood.

FOURTH SUMMER ON. Laterals and sub-laterals are treated as for third summer. The leader is allowed to continue, but when maximum height is reached the buds at the top of the leader are rubbed out in spring as they begin to develop. This prevents unwanted growth for which no space is available. ·

55. Overcrowded spurs and growths which should be thinned out in December.

Deshooting (*Disbudding*)

The purpose of this operation is to restrict growths produced to one per spur. For the unskilled gardener it is safest to wait until grape bunches (i.e. flower trusses) show and then break off carefully with thumb and forefinger all the unwanted shoots with the smaller, weaker bunches, some perhaps with no flower at all. Those laterals remaining are then pinched at two leaves beyond the bunch of grapes, as already described.

This annual attention to pruning detail has considerable influence on the regular fruiting of the vine, coupled with other points to be mentioned below. Without pruning and disbudding a tangled mass of weakened shoots results and the size and quality of the bunches of grapes soon falls off.

Fruiting

Overcropping a vine at any stage in its life is asking for trouble, but especially so in the early years. For a vine in average health and vigour the crop taken should not exceed one bunch per foot of rod. Many more bunches than required may often begin to develop, but these must be removed, as already mentioned (under 'Deshooting').

56. Grape-thinning. (*Left*) The unthinned bunch. (*Right*) After thinning.

Thinning the Fruit

Where large fruits are required some thinning of the fruit will be necessary (Pl. 56). Basically this involves cutting out with scissors those berries lying awkwardly 'inside' the general shape of the bunch. This gives the outer fruit more light and space in which to develop to the full. Thinning can be started as soon as berries begin swelling. Heavy thinning should be avoided at first, and final spacing should preferably be reached in two operations, i.e. thin the obvious 'non-starters' first and follow up with a second thinning once it can be seen how a bunch is developing.

Feeding

This need not normally amount to much for outdoor vines. A light mulch of well-rotted manure over the whole border in spring would be ideal but should be withheld where experience shows that growth is already over-vigorous. Feeding is particularly necessary where cropping has been heavy or where growth is obviously lacking.

Watering

Borders against walls and fences are frequently drier than the rest of the garden and it is important to water well and in good time. Beware the moist-surfaced border beneath which the soil is dust dry. Adequate moisture is particularly necessary as growth starts, so that a check should be made from March or April onwards.

Cultivars

Comparatively few outdoor grapes are offered by nurserymen simply because the crop is not widely grown. What is interesting is that the cultivars usually obtainable are in many instances not considered to be in the running in Mr Barrington Brock's estimation. Two short lists are therefore included. The first is of those grapes frequently listed in catalogues, the second of Mr Barrington Brock's own select choice as quoted in *Fruit – Present and Future* (see p. 174).

A. Outdoor Grapes Listed in Current Catalogues

NOIR HATIF DE MARSEILLES. Small black grapes with good muscat flavour; early.

PERLE DE CZABA. Ripen consistently but growth is often poor.

PRECOCE DE SAUMUR (MUSCAT DE SAUMUR). Golden grapes of good muscat flavour but cropping indifferent; early.

STRAWBERRY. An American hybrid. Primarily of value for its autumn colour. Small black grape with a faint trace of strawberry flavour.

BRANT. A Canadian grape. Fair flavour, late ripening. Good autumn colour.

BLACK HAMBURG. A well-known black grape. Fair flavour.

B. Outdoor Grapes recommended by Mr Barrington Brock

MARSHAL JOFFRE. French. A promising new introduction.

NOIR HATIF DE MARSEILLES. Fairly small black grape with slight muscat flavour. One of the best for the open.

SIEGERREBE. Ripens dark brown, early.

PIROVANO 14. Ripens deep reddish black. A good eating grape; ripens early.

OLIVER IRSAY. Hungarian. Ripens white with muscat flavour. Mid-season.

EXCELSIOR. French. Easily grown. Ripens white, flavour fair only.

BRANT. As above.

As comparison will show, only two grapes are common to both lists – 'Noir Hatif de Marseilles' and 'Brant'.

Pests

There are no major pests of vines growing in the open.

Diseases

Mildew can be troublesome where site conditions are excessively dry and thus conducive to the disease. White patches are most conspicuous on the leaves, but shoots, flowers and fruits may also be affected.

Control. It is important to spray with dinocap at the first sign of this disease, repeating the treatment as often as required. Well-spaced growth helps to reduce the possibility of the disease occurring.

14 · Propagation

Healthy Stock

Chapter 3 highlights the reason for withholding unqualified support for the garden propagation of soft fruits. When one considers that the most popular of these – strawberry, raspberry and blackcurrant – are all prone to serious virus diseases it will be seen why one is wary of encouraging widespread garden propagation. Nevertheless there is no reason at all why the informed gardener should not propagate his own plants and so save himself the expense of buying in fresh stock *where he is certain that his material is healthy.*

Free-Cropping Clones

There is not only the health angle to consider. Of equal importance is the desirability of having a free-cropping strain or clone. Obviously one should always select those specimens with the best cropping record and propagate from them. Such plants or bushes should be marked, for it may be several months before propagation is done and one bush looks uncommonly like the next if it has no identification label.

Site

If for reasons beyond one's control propagation cannot be done without diseased material being within close proximity, the advisability of raising new plants – or indeed of buying in new ones – is certainly open to question.

Soil

Ground that has been well worked as garden soil for a number of years is the kind to choose. It has the depth and texture for rapid rooting and sufficient humus and plant nutrients to sustain the young plants until they are ready for moving to their permanent quarters. For preference choose soil that has not grown the crop being propagated. There is then less likelihood of any soil-borne troubles being encountered.

Soil that is too wet will not be suitable; sandy soils on the other hand may be ideal for rooting cuttings providing these are not allowed to suffer from drought. This is an important point, for losses in spring of apparently successfully rooted cuttings can be severe if the cutting bed is allowed to dry out. In dry springs watering may be necessary as early as April.

On the heavier, yet not too wet, clay soils the incorporation of peat and sand (up to $\frac{1}{8}$ in. grist) at the base of cutting trenches can help considerably.

Weed Control

Clean ground is an obvious necessity and if any of the more serious perennial nuisances like couch or bindweed are encountered the use of the ground for propagation should be questioned. It is probably wisest not to use herbicides around propagation material.

Manures and Fertilizers

In general these should not be used, certainly not for cuttings. Strawberry runners usually benefit from the digging-in of a little well-rotted manure or compost before the parent plants are put in.

Strawberries

Propagation is very simple and this is why it is necessary to be doubly careful when raising or accepting homegrown runners. The practice of selecting runners from fruiting beds is not a sound one – it is much safer to grow one or two plants well away from any others purely for runner production. Ideally, start with bought-in certified runners. Save one or two of the best for runner production, keep them deblossomed and keep the runners from each plant isolated from the next. By doing this it is easy to dig up and burn any plant that shows virus disease symptoms *together with all its runners*, which will also be infected. Each autumn two or three runners are planted to repeat the process for as long as the stock remains healthy. With any luck this may be for two or three seasons, after which fresh certified stock should again be obtained.

For ease of planting, runners can be pinned onto and rooted into small 3–3$\frac{1}{2}$ in. pots of compost partially sunk into the soil. It is best to treat the first-formed runners in this way so that they are available as early as possible for planting in August.

Pests and Diseases

Routine precautions are most important against aphids (see p. 65) and mildew (see p. 69). The aphids may well bring in virus that will quickly ruin the stock, and mildew can spoil a promising runner bed.

Raspberries

If your existing canes are definitely healthy and vigorous there is no reason why you should not propagate from them. To do this is very simple – the suckers, instead of being hoed off are allowed to develop and the best are lifted and planted in the autumn (see p. 77 for instructions on planting). It must be realized however that many garden raspberries are virus-infected (Pl. 22, p. 91) and unless one is absolutely certain that the plants are full of health, vigour and cropping potential it is pointless to propagate from them.

Blackberries and Loganberries

The remarks concerning virus diseases under raspberries apply equally here. Again propagation is simple, this time by tip-layering. In late June, July and August the new canes should be long enough to bend over in order to *bury* the tips in the soil. Some compost worked in, if necessary, will make it friable, and it must also be moist. Heavy soils are definitely less suitable. First make a vertical nick in the soil approximately at a point where the tip is to be buried. Next insert the spade at 45° and take out a block of soil to meet the first upright cut. The cane tip is then laid into the hole along the sloping 'floor' and covered by about 6 ins. of soil, which is carefully firmed.

By the autumn the tip layer should normally have rooted (Pl. 57). It is wisest to leave it undisturbed until late winter or early spring before moving it to its permanent site. The cane is then cut about a foot from the tip, which forms a convenient 'handle'. If the roots are not considered adequate it is better to grow the layer on for a season and plant a year later.

Mention must be made of another method of propagating these fruits where a lot of new plants are required and material is very limited. This is the method of using leaf-bud cuttings

163

57. Rooted blackberry from a shoot tip-layered earlier in the summer. Loganberry and other hybrid berries can be propagated in the same way.

whereby *each bud* on each cane, except those at the still soft tip, will produce a new plant. A frame or propagating bench is necessary, and a little heat beneficial though by no means essential. The cuttings are prepared in the period June–September and are carefully cut out much as a rose or apple bud for budding. In this case, however, *the leaf remains intact*, complete with bud and 'heel' of stem. The tiny cuttings are then inserted 4 ins. apart in a sandy, peaty mixture with only the top of the leaf showing. The frame is kept shut after the cuttings have been watered in and shading will be required from direct sun. The cuttings must be watered but not too much or they will rot. As rooting begins (usually in three to four weeks) a crack of ventilation can be given, and this should be gradually increased as the weeks go by. After two months or so the cuttings should have rooted. They are then transferred to a nursery bed to grow on for a further year before planting out.

The above method is seldom necessary in the garden but could well be useful with a hybrid berry that proves difficult to root from tip layers.

Blackcurrants

Propagation is easy, but the health of the parent bushes must be beyond question. Big bud mite (Pl. 30, p. 113) and reversion virus (Pl. 33, p. 117) are not hard to find, and there are probably far more unhealthy garden blackcurrants than healthy ones. Therefore be quite certain that the cuttings are from clean bushes.

Blackcurrants are propagated by hardwood cuttings taken from sturdy, well-ripened shoots formed earlier in the summer (Pl. 58). Given good soil conditions the cuttings will root like weeds and a 100 per cent 'take' or rooting is commonplace Sandy soils produce particularly good results; heavier, wetter ones may cause a little trouble. The time of taking the cuttings is important, the latter half of September and October being the best period. The shoots are cut from the bushes; the leaves are carefully removed, together with the soft shoot tips. The cuttings are then made, 8–10 ins. long, with a cut just above the top bud and near to a bud at the base (although the latter is often unnecessary). *All buds must remain on the cutting intact* (Pls. 58, 59). It is from these that regular supplies of young shoots will form in later years – essential if blackcurrants are to be grown well.

The cuttings are inserted into a straight-backed trench to a depth which will leave, *at the most*, two buds showing above ground (Pl. 59). The trench can be easily taken out with a spade against a garden line. Cuttings are spaced 8–9 ins. apart, with rows at least 2 ft apart if for some reason that quantity is required. Soil is replaced a little at a time and thoroughly firmed over the whole length of the cutting. It is important to firm the cuttings well after sharp frost.

Growth the following season on average garden soils should be more than adequate. The one-year-old bushes can then be moved to their permanent quarters (i.e. a year from the cutting being taken), although two-year bushes are often better for planting (Pl. 25, p. 104). If growth has been poor, cut all shoots to ground level during the winter and grow on for a further year.

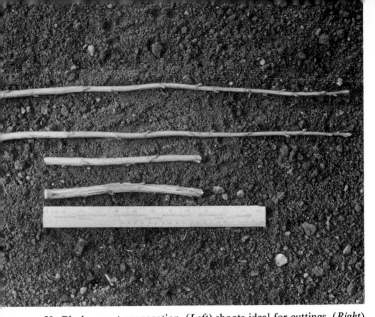

58. Blackcurrant propagation. (*Left*) shoots ideal for cuttings. (*Right*) The cuttings made.

59. Blackcurrant cuttings being inserted.

60. Red and white currant propagation. (*Left*) Shoots ideal for cuttings. (*Right*) The cuttings made, with lower buds removed.

61. Gooseberry cuttings being inserted.

If it is suspected or known that the poor growth has been due to unhealthy cuttings then the plants should be dug up and burnt.

Pests

Big bud mite (blackcurrant gall mite) is always a danger and the lime sulphur treatment advocated on p. 112 should include any cuttings or young bushes still in cutting beds, first spraying them just after growth has started.

Red and White Currants

For the most part these are as easy to root from cuttings as blackcurrants. Often, however, 'Rivers' Late Red' is slower to root than most other cultivars.

Cuttings are taken in late September–October from well-ripened shoots of the current year's growth. Long shoots will be necessary – cuttings should be 12 ins. in length, even 14 or 15 ins. if possible (Pl. 60). The extra length is necessary because the red or white currant bush is grown on a stem. An important variation from blackcurrant cuttings is that *all lower buds are rubbed off*, leaving only the top three or four. This ensures a clean-stemmed bush free from any unwanted sucker shoots.

The cuttings are inserted so that one half their length is below soil level (cf. Pl. 61), spacing is 8–9 ins. in the rows and at least 2 ft apart, 2 ft 6 ins. if possible. Firming the cuttings after frost should also be done as required – in case they have been loosened.

Good red and white currant cuttings should produce three strong shoots during the summer, but this will depend on good growing conditions (Pl. 34, p. 122). At the end of the first year the one-year or maiden plants can be moved to their permanent quarter if they are robust enough. If in any doubt it is best to leave them undisturbed for a further season. In either event it is important to prune them hard back to three buds or so, as described on p. 123.

Gooseberries

These are far more difficult to propagate from cuttings than blackcurrants or redcurrants, and the use of a rooting hormone is advisable. It seems that a number of variable factors cause the very inconsistent results so often experienced: the type of wood the cutting is made from, the time of taking the cutting, soil and weather conditions – all these, or rather a combination of them, appear to determine whether there is a good take or not. Generally speaking it is best to take cuttings early, in mid-late September and October. Experiments have borne this out. Shoots used should be vigorous, straight and well-ripened and the top inch or two should always be removed – not only may it be soft, it may also be infected with American gooseberry mildew (Pl. 50, p. 147).

The actual cuttings are made and inserted in exactly the same way as for red and white currants – 12 ins. long at least, and with all basal buds removed (thorns too if required (Pls. 60, 61).

Leaves will still be on the shoots in September–October and these are carefully pulled off before cuttings are inserted. Growth in the first year is often not good, and it is therefore advisable to leave the cuttings undisturbed for two seasons before moving them. They should still be pruned hard to encourage strong growth, as described on p. 134.

Disease

American gooseberry mildew is often troublesome and it is best to spray cuttings regularly with dinocap (or lime sulphur where varieties will tolerate it).

Blueberries

The easiest way of propagation is by layering. Suitably placed shoots are pulled down and pegged in position into the soil in the autumn, and by the following autumn should have rooted. An alternative method is to plant cuttings in a closed frame – a mist unit in a greenhouse is ideal. The cuttings are taken in July, about 3 ins. long and from semi-hardened side shoots.

Grape Vines

The majority of these can be raised easily from cuttings inserted in the open ground in February.

15 · Weed Control

The satisfactory cultivation of soft fruits requires, among other things, an adequate control of weeds. This is something that is seldom achieved. Competition from weeds for plant foods and moisture means that in many gardens only a fraction of the potential soft-fruit crop is ever realized.

Annual weeds like groundsel and chickweed that grow, flower, seed and die in quick profusion are a nuisance but do not present the serious problems that are posed by a build-up of some of the perennials. Two or three come to mind immediately – couch ('twitch', 'scutch', 'stroil') and convolvulus ('bindweed') in particular – but ground elder, docks, creeping thistle, bryony and creeping buttercup also can and will multiply quickly where conditions suit them. Bushes and canes become choked and growth and cropping soon suffer in consequence.

Clean Ground for Planting

This requirement is a *must*. It is much wiser to delay planting for a year rather than to plant on dirty ground. Detailed preparation is fully discussed in Chapter 5, pp. 36–38. Possibly the easiest course is to use a suitable herbicide to clean the vacant ground; this point is covered on p. 172.

Hoeing

Light, regular hoeing to prevent weed seedlings developing is the quickest and easiest remedy. Once weed growth develops it is hard work to remove it and if suitable herbicides are used it is often difficult to avoid the bushes themselves when applying them. The temptation to dig or use a mechanical cultivator through established soft-fruit crops must be resisted. It leads to substantial root damage as well as unnecessary root disturbance and may also increase the risk of drought conditions. Hoe lightly during dry weather when the weeds are small and they will shrivel in a matter of minutes. The dutch or push hoe is the best tool for the job, but it must be sufficiently sharp to cut the weed roots cleanly.

Garden Cultivators

The value of garden cultivators among soft fruits is limited. There is no doubt that the best method of preparing ground for small-scale planting is that of thorough digging. However, in the breaking-up of the soil surface to a good tilth before planting mechanical cultivators can be of great assistance.

Mulching

The benefit of surface mulches is stressed over and over again under each fruit in turn. Not least does their value lie in smothering the soil surface so that potential weeds are unable to develop beyond the germination stage. There is no doubt that where sufficient material can be found to give a covering of about 3 ins., this is the most desirable method of weed control, coupled as it is with the conservation of soil moisture and the provision of small amounts of plant nutrients. Mulching is fully discussed in Chapter 5, p. 41.

Herbicides Among Soft Fruits

The care and precision called for in the use of herbicides among growing crops means that in general manufacturers cannot safely recommend their use for this purpose by amateur gardeners. This explains why so many products advertised for use by commercial growers are not available through retail channels. The risk, as things are at present, would be too great. In due course it is likely that more and more specific formulations of herbicides may become available for use among garden crops.

Currently, attention is drawn to the following two chemicals for use among soft fruits:

1. PARAQUAT. This is already available to gardeners under a well-known proprietary name. It is a contact herbicide, killing only those parts of the plant that it actually touches. Annual weeds are usually destroyed, but deep-rooted perennials may require two or three applications for reasonable control. Paraquat is therefore an ideal herbicide for use among garden soft fruits providing none is spilt or allowed to *drift* onto the crops

themselves or, indeed, on to neighbours' plants. This is particularly important for crops such as blackcurrants and blueberries, where basal buds can be damaged by spray drift, even when dormant.

2. SIMAZINE. This chemical also has for some time been available for use by amateurs under certain proprietary names. Directions however are normally for use on paths and waste ground, not (as in commercial horticulture) among soft fruits. This is because it must be applied very accurately and at the right time; also application rates vary depending on the type of soil and its condition. Thus it would be difficult to quote rates that the general public could safely work on. Any amateur gardener contemplating the use of simazine among soft fruits would be well advised to write to the manufacturers for specific advice.

Simazine is a residual type of herbicide and so its effects are felt for some months following application. It must be used on clean ground, its purpose being to kill weeds as they germinate.

Herbicides on Vacant Ground

This poses a different problem. Apparently easier to solve, it is necessary, even so, to exercise care. The herbicide may, for instance, be washed by heavy rain onto lower levels.

There are a number of chemical herbicides readily available to gardeners for the express purpose of clearing waste ground. Paraquat is undoubtedly one of the easiest and safest (see p. 171), but it may require two or three consecutive applications to kill perennial weeds. Simazine may also be used, taking care to apply it at the correct rate. In fact simazine and paraquat used together can be most efficient. Where couch grass is the chief problem dalapon should be tried, because this is its specific use. Sodium chlorate is a time-honoured remedy, but it must not be applied too close to trees, shrubs and other plants, or they too may be killed. Moreover it can take up to a year for ground to return to a safe state for planting after sodium chlorate treatment.

Probably the best test to see if soil is suitable for planting following herbicide treatment is to sow a sensitive annual crop like lettuce or radish. If they germinate and grow satisfactorily this is usually an indication that no side-effects of the herbicide

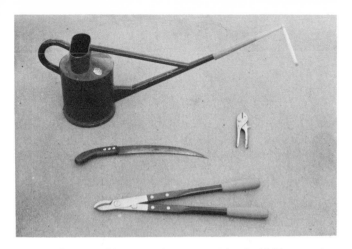

62. Watering-can with weeder bar for applying herbicides, pruning saw, pruning shears, and secateurs.

remain. Makers' instructions should indicate the approximate waiting period.

Application of Herbicides

This calls for care and common sense. Used correctly weedkillers (to give herbicides the name by which they are more widely known in gardening circles) are a considerable asset, but in the wrong hands they can cause serious damage. They should never be used among or near crops on a windy day.

Firstly, it must be ensured that the correct weedkiller is being used for the purpose in hand. Paraquat on a lawn, for example, would be disastrous. Equally so would a selective weed-killer for lawns be among soft fruits.

For garden purposes the safest appliance for weedkillers is a watering can with a rose. The 'spray' droplets from the rose are large and are unlikely to drift onto other plants. In fact special spray bars (Pl. 62) are obtainable for watering cans. Knapsack sprayers (Pl. 6, p. 34) are an alternative, but there is more risk of drift here.

It is important to calibrate or measure the application of a herbicide accurately. If instructions state that the mixture should be used at the rate of, say, 1 gallon to 50 square yards, this must be adhered to. The easiest method is to have a dummy run with water first. A finer rose or nozzle setting may be necessary, or a coarser one. Equally, it may be necessary to quicken one's pace of coverage. Experimenting with plain water is well worthwhile, so that the herbicide is applied as perfectly and accurately as possible. To sum up, the precautions to take are:

1. Ensure that the right chemical is being used for the purpose required.

2. Ensure that makers' instructions are followed step by step.

3. Ensure that cans or sprayers are kept specifically for the use of herbicides, preferably marking them clearly 'WEEDKILLERS ONLY'. If used later for other purposes (e.g. watering or spraying) traces of certain herbicides can easily damage plants.

4. Ensure that the spray of herbicide does not drift in the wind. Avoid windy days for such work.

5. Ensure that receptacles are thoroughly washed out in a safe manner. Do not for example swill out in a water tank used for watering plants.

Soft Fruits Overgrown with Weed

Where soft fruits have become badly overgrown with weed it is usually wisest to grub them up and consign them to the bonfire. The vacant ground can then be treated accordingly, possibly using a suitable herbicide, before replanting. Ideally, however, a fresh site should be chosen, if only for a change of soil (see also Chapter 16).

Readers are particularly referred to the following specialist publications on herbicides for general guidance:

Chemicals for the Gardener, Ministry of Agriculture Booklet, from H.M.S.O., York House, Kingsway, London WC2 (1s. 3d.)

Gardening Chemicals, from The Secretary, R.H.S. Offices, Vincent Square, London SW1 (7s. 6d. plus 9d. postage).

Fruit – Present and Future (which contains an article 'Chemical Weed Control in the Garden' by D. W. Robinson) published by the Royal Horticultural Society, now out of print, but worth borrowing from a library.

16 · Neglected Soft Fruits

It could be argued that there is little point in devoting space to this subject when plants which have been neglected are such a bad risk. Certainly this should be the general attitude, for in the long run a fresh start on newly prepared ground will bring quicker and more certain results. Neglected plants and bushes may well be harbouring pests and diseases, not to mention incurable virus troubles. They will almost certainly be starved and choked by heavy weed growth, and once this has occurred it is very difficult, often impossible, to clean the area thoroughly.

Perhaps the best way of assessing the possibilities of overgrown soft-fruit plants is to consider the following points:

1. *Health*

If there is any doubt at all about the health of a neglected plant or bush it is wisest to dispense with it. Obviously there will be instances where temporary troubles (e.g. damage from caterpillars or capsids) can be overcome, but where more serious pests and diseases, like dieback on currants and gooseberries, big bud or virus diseases, are apparent it is a mistake to retain such material (Pls. 4, 22, 30).

2. *Site*

The plants may have deteriorated because they occupy an unfavourable position, and this should not be overlooked. Exposure to wind or draughts and excessive shading are typical examples of this. One that occurs frequently is the man-made 'wind tunnel' between two properties, which seems to draw the wind and makes successful gardening a problem. It may be difficult to obtain a consistently good set of fruit in such situations and many young shoots may be broken off in gusty summer breezes. While several of the soft fruits will succeed in partial shade, planting too close to large trees is frequently a waste of time. Growth becomes drawn and one-sided (Pl. 2) and cropping suffers in consequence.

3. *Soil*

Considerations here are parallel to those for site. If results are to be consistently good, both site and soil must be suitable – they are fundamental to success (Chapters 1 and 2). The heavy clay soils which lack good drainage are the likeliest bar to success, but mismanagement on thin soils that dry out quickly can be equally devastating. Soft-fruit plants must grow steadily during the summer so that the foundations for future crops can be soundly laid.

Obviously, if soil conditions are suspect it is a waste of time trying to renovate plants that are already struggling because of them. It is better to select an alternative site where the soil can be improved during preparation as necessary (see p. 18).

4. *Age of Plants/Bushes*

If strawberries are a tangled mass, currants weak and gnarled and gooseberry bushes a thicket of suckers (Pl. 63) one can be sure that the plants are already a good age. They can of course still be productive after a good many years, but by the time they have been cleaned up, pruned and revived much better results would have been obtained from young, newly planted stock.

Young plants are an entirely different proposition, and providing they are healthy they may be well worth persevering with.

5. *Cultivars (Varieties)*

A natural exception to the previous point is that of out-of-date cultivars. New ones may not always stand the test of time, but it is quite possible that old stock is inferior in fruit size, weight of crop and possibly, though not necessarily, in quality and flavour in the crops it produces. To a large extent this is a matter of personal choice. A check with friends and neighbours may soon show old stock to be an uneconomic proposition.

6. *Weeds*

Annual weeds and grass present no major obstacle that cultivation and/or the use of herbicides cannot overcome. On the other hand if rampant pernicious *perennials* like bindweed (convolvulus), couch grass or ground elder have become firmly established, it may well be easiest in the long run to start afresh. Herbicides to cure such ills are easily available to the com-

63. Suckers at the base of a gooseberry bush. If not removed from the point of origin they will quickly multiply.

mercial grower but not to the general public. These are fully discussed in Chapter 15.

Having checked on the above points it should not be difficult to decide whether or not existing soft fruits warrant cleaning-up and general renovation. If they do it may be useful briefly to explain the treatment the individual fruits usually require.

Strawberries

Unless the plants are really vigorous the wisest course with strawberries is to dispense with them and start afresh. Should existing plants appear to be strong and healthy, however, select the strongest runners and plant these on freshly prepared ground in August–September. If virus shows itself (see p. 70) then the whole stock, including escapes in grass, must be dug up and burnt and a fresh start made with certified virus-free plants.

Raspberries, Loganberries, Blackberries, etc.

General weakness may be the problem here through competition from weeds and grass. Firstly, remove all weed as far as possible, then prune out all the old dead and fruited canes, leaving the strongest young ones. This will give access to further weed growth, which can in turn be removed. A good mulch of rotted farmyard manure should then be given, plus fertilizers if necessary (see p. 36).

If in spite of such treatment growth and crops remain disappointing the answer is clear, particularly as virus diseases are a major problem in raspberries (Pl. 22, p. 91).

Blackcurrants

Neglected bushes (Pls. 4, 30) are seldom worth the bother of renovation, as they are usually carrying big bud and reversion. If they happen by good fortune to be healthy the area should be generally cleaned up and then mulched heavily in early April with well-rotted farmyard manure. The most important part of the operation is drastic pruning. The bush is simply cut down *completely* in winter to buds just above ground level, where these are visible. Such treatment may seem so severe as to be ridiculous, but it is nevertheless correct and is identical to that necessary for newly planted bushes (see p. 105).

If worthwhile crops are not forthcoming within two seasons (allowing for spring frosts) the health of the bushes should be questioned and expert advice sought. Most important of all, new certified bushes should be procured for any fresh planting and not plants raised by cuttings from the unsatisfactory parents.

Red and White Currants

Big bud and reversion are not as serious a problem here as they are with blackcurrants, but bird damage may have seriously denuded the branches of fruiting spurs. If so the bonfire is the answer.

Younger bushes containing plenty of spurs should have the ground around them cleaned and fed (see p. 120). They will also require careful winter pruning to reduce and shorten the overgrown and weakened spur systems. The cutting to the ground recommended for blackcurrants is of no use here because of the habit of red and white currants of fruiting year after year on the same branches. The centre of the bush should be opened up and the strongest and youngest branches retained up to a maximum of about eight in number.

Large pruning wounds are best sealed to reduce the incidence of dieback disease.

Gooseberries

These offer perhaps the best chance of success where old bushes are found. Providing too many buds have not been lost through winter bird damage, and suckers (Pl. 63) do not pose an insurmountable problem (by recurring and multiplying annually), there is no reason why healthy old bushes should not again be productive. If on the other hand growth is sparse or suckers are rampant, it is best to start afresh, preferably with young stock of named sorts from a reliable source.

To renovate old bushes the first step should be to remove unwanted branches and growths. Any that are too low or crowded should be cut out, the aim being to obtain an open-centred bush with well-spaced branches. In subsequent seasons more detailed spur pruning should be carried out (see pp. 134–5). Branches are best removed with a pruning saw and wounds sealed with a fungicidal tree paint.

Blueberries

Mulching with peat plus a sprinkling of sulphate of ammonia is well worth trying. Old worn-out shoots should be cut out in winter, but if bushes do not quickly respond with new growth then fresh stock should be obtained.

Vines

Overgrown specimens can be pruned quite drastically providing they are completely dormant. This means pruning in December to early January. Side growths should be cut away to within two buds of the original rod (Pls. 53, 55). It is important to cut to a visible bud, otherwise a fresh break of growth is unlikely to develop. The border should be fed on the lines described on p. 158.

Having summarized the treatment required, it only remains to emphasize two most important points. These are:

1. *Pest and disease control* – which must be attended to sensibly. A tar-oil winter wash on everything except strawberries should be the first and thereafter annual routine, and if this is backed up by the one or two other vital sprays necessary (e.g. lime sulphur for big bud on blackcurrants, derris on raspberries against raspberry beetle, etc. etc.) much will have been done towards the successful rehabilitation of soft fruits.

2. *Replanting on a fresh site* – which is not always easy in the small garden, but is well worth doing. For one thing the ground will be in need of a change of crop and, more important, certain virus and other troubles can be carried in the soil in certain instances. Fresh ground will almost certainly give better results.

17 · Recipe for Success

Let it be said unhesitatingly that soft fruits *are* well worth growing. They will not fall victim to *all* the troubles *all* the time; frost will *not* ruin the crop every year and where one fruit may struggle another may well succeed.

British Standards

Looking to the future, attention must be drawn to British Standard specifications for fruit trees, bushes and plants bought from nurserymen. These specifications have been drawn up by the British Standards Institution as a guide both to nurserymen and to the general public on what standards particular trees and bushes should reach. This is something that will be an invaluable guide to amateur gardeners, who may have no idea what is or what is not a good specimen when they buy fresh stock. The publication in question, British Standard 3936, Part 3, *Fruit Specification for Nursery Stock*, is available from British Standards Institution, British Standards House, 2 Park Street, London w1 (5s.).

'Expert Advice'

In conclusion, a word about seeking 'expert advice'. It is easy to advise this, but it is often impossible for the gardener to know where he can apply for it. Sources for such information would certainly include:

1. County Horticultural Education Officers. Not all counties maintain such a service, but where such exist they are usually based at the County Hall of the county in question.

2. County Horticultural Advisory Officers. Every county is covered by this service, which is part of the National Agricultural Advisory Service of the Ministry of Agriculture, but it is run specifically for the *commercial grower*.

3. The Royal Horticultural Society's Garden, Wisley, Ripley, Woking, Surrey. The R.H.S. maintain an advisory service for the benefit of Fellows of the Society .

4. The horticultural press.

The trouble taken in obtaining expert advice on soft fruit growing will usually pay good dividends.

Appendix · Ministry of Agriculture Publications

These bulletins and advisory leaflets have been written primarily for the commercial fruit-grower, but contain information of much value to the amateur.

BULLETINS
Bush Fruits, 4
Strawberries, 95
Cane Fruits, 156

ADVISORY LEAFLETS
Blackcurrants, 543
Gooseberries, 215
Loganberries, 129
Raspberries, 180
Red currants, 521
Bryobia Mites, 305
Coral Spot, 23
Currant and Gooseberry Aphids, 176
Currant and Gooseberry Sawflies, 30
Eelworms on Strawberries, 414
Gooseberry Powdery Mildew, 273
Magpie Moth, 65
Mussel Scale and Brown Scale, 88
Raspberry Beetle, 164
Raspberry Moth, 66
Red Core of Strawberries, 410
Reversion Disease and Gall Mite on Blackcurrants, 277
Virus Diseases of Strawberry, 530
Wingless Weevils, 57

Index